THE MULTICULTURAL WORKSHOP

BOOK 3

Linda Lonon Blanton
Linda Lee

Heinle & Heinle Publishers

I(T)P   An International Thomson Publishing Company

Pacific Grove • Albany • Bonn • Boston • Cincinnati • Detroit • London • Madrid • Melbourne
Mexico City • New York • Paris • San Francisco • Tokyo • Toronto • Washington

Heinle & Heinle Publishers
20 Park Plaza
Boston, MA 02116 U.S.A.

International Thomson
  Publishing
Berkshire House 168-173
High Holborn
London WC1V7AA
England

Thomas Nelson Australia
102 Dodds Street
South Melbourne, 3205
Victoria, Australia

Nelson Canada
1120 Birchmont Road
Scarborough, Ontario
Canada M1K5G4

International Thomson
  Publishing Gmbh
Königwinterer Strasse 418
53227 Bonn
Germany

International Thomson
  Publishing Asia
Block 211 Henderson Road
  #08-03
Henderson Industrial Park
Singapore 0315

International Thomson
  Publishing–Japan
Hirakawacho-cho Kyowa
  Building, 3F
2-2-1 Hirakawacho-cho
Chiyoda-ku, 102 Tokyo
Japan

The publication of *The Multicultural Workshop: Book 3* was directed by the members of the Newbury House Publishing Team at Heinle & Heinle:

Erik Gundersen, Editorial Director
John F. McHugh, Market Development Director
Kristin Thalheimer, Production Services Coordinator
Elizabeth Holthaus, Director of Production and Team Leader

Also participating in the publication of this program were:

Publisher: Stanley J. Galek
Project Manager: Angela Malovich Castro, English Language Trainers
Assistant Editor: Karen P. Hazar
Production Assistant: Maryellen Eschmann
Manufacturing Coordinator: Mary Beth Hennebury
Interior Designer and Compositor: Greta D. Sibley
Illustrators: Normand Cousineau, Anne O'Brien, Stephanie Peterson
Cover Artist: Alan Witschonke
Cover Designer: Bortman Design Group
Cover Typographer: James Steinberg
Photo Researcher: Philippe Heckly

Library of Congress Cataloging-in-Publication Data
Blanton, Linda Lonon, 1942–
      The multicultural workshop.

      1. English language--Textbooks for foreign speakers.
I. Lee, Linda.   II. Title.
PE1128.B59215   1994   428.2'4   93-39447
ISBN 0-8384-4834-8 (v. 1)
ISBN 0-8384-4835-6 (v. 2)
ISBN 0-8384-5020-2 (v. 3)

A Special Thanks

The authors and publisher would like to thank the following individuals who reviewed and/or field-tested *The Multicultural Workshop: Book 3* at various stages of its development and who offered many helpful insights and suggestions:

Judith L. Paiva, *Northern Virginia Community College*

Cheryl Benz, *Miami-Dade Community College*

Brad Stocker, *Miami-Dade Community College*

Lorin Leith, *Santa Rosa Junior College (CA)*

Joe McVeigh, *California State University, Los Angeles*

Heather Robertson, *California State University, Los Angeles*

Tom Coles, *Arizona State University*

Adrianne Saltz, *Boston University*

Jamie Beaton, *Boston University*

John Dennis, *San Francisco State University, Emeritus*

Virginia Herringer, *Pasadena City College*

Virginia Gibbons, *Oakton Community College (IL)*

Danielle Dibie, *California State University, Northridge*

Helen Harper, *American Language Institute, New York University*

Bernadette Garcia Budd, *Suffolk County Community College (NJ)*

Julietta Ruppert, *Houston Community College*

Elizabeth Templin, *University of Arizona*

Charles Schroen, *The Pennsylvania State University*

Betty Speyrer, *Delgado Community College (LA)*

Marjorie Vai, *The New School for Social Research*

Marianne Phinney, *University of Texas, El Paso*

Eve Chambers Sanchez, *Oregon State University*

Vivian Wind Aronow, *College of Staten Island (City University of New York)*

Luke Bailey, *University of Hawaii at Hilo*

Martha Low, *University of Oregon*

Virginia Vogel Zanger, *Boston University*

Lois Spitzer, *Atlantic Community College (NJ)*

Fredericka Stoller, *Northern Arizona University*

Wendy Hyman-Fite, *Washington University in St. Louis*

Peggy Anderson, *Wichita State University*

Pat Holdcraft, *University of Miami*

Kim Smith, *University of Texas, Austin*

Sally LaLuzerne-Oi, *Hawaii Pacific University*

Elizabeth Byleen, *University of Kansas*

Mac Toll, *Colorado School of Mines & University of Colorado at Boulder*

Meredith Pike-Baky, *University of California, Berkeley & San Francisco Unified School District*

CONTENTS

GUIDE TO STRATEGIES

The Multicultural Workshop *Program*

The Multicultural Workshop is a fully integrated reading and writing program for students of English as a Second Language. It is based on an interactive pedagogy that values collaboration and meaningful communication as powerful tools for learning. In practice, the program takes the form of classroom activities in which students discuss, read, and write together—always within a thematic context that provides topical substance and linguistic coherence.

The Multicultural Workshop: Book 3 is designed for intermediate/low-advanced ESL students. The series begins with *Book 1,* which lays a foundation for the critical literacy students need for academic study. *Books 2* and *3* continue building as students become more involved in the kinds of reading and writing required of them in the academic mainstream.

While the same five themes—**identity, change, choices, relationships**, and **conflict**—integrate the series, the focus within a given thematic area shifts from book to book. For example, in *Book 1,* students focus on **change** as an individual phenomenon; in *Book 2,* **change** is analyzed as an environmental process; in *Book 3,* the theme of **change** is viewed through a social and political perspective. The format allows integration and a growing sophistication in students' work.

A resource box containing over a hundred readings is an integral part of the program. Designed to bring the library into the classroom, the box holds laminated reading cards, charts for recording students' progress through the box, and answer keys to questions about the readings. Graded by level of difficulty, the readings range from a level easily accessible to students using *Book 1* to fairly challenging for students using *Book 3.* In other words, no matter which book of the series students are working in, they will find plenty of additional readings in the resource box.

We are grateful to Erik Gundersen, Editor for College/Intensive ESL at Heinle & Heinle, and to Karen Hazar, Assistant Editor, for their help. Both have gone out of their way to assist us in getting the program together. We also want to thank Betty Speyrer, a teacher at Delgado Community College in New Orleans, whose students taught us a lot about the *The Multicultural Workshop.*

The Multicultural Workshop: Book 3 is a reading and writing program for students of English as a Second Language at a high-intermediate/low-advanced level of proficiency. Like the other books in the series, *Book 3* is based on an interactive pedagogy that values collaboration and meaningful communication as powerful tools for learning. In practice, the pedagogy takes the form of classroom activities in which students discuss, read, and write together—always within a thematic context.

Overview

❖ **GOALS.** *The Multicultural Workshop: Book 3* is designed to do the following:

- increase students' overall fluency in English

- raise students' reading and writing proficiencies

- increase students' vocabulary

- help students develop strategies for critical thinking, reading, and writing

- promote the acquisition of critical literacy, required for students' success in future academic study.

Field testing has shown us that ESL students using *The Multicultural Workshop* acquire an eagerness to participate in their own learning; an awareness of their individual responsibility as readers and writers in the communication process; and an understanding of the essential role of their own insights and experience in responding to others' texts and in producing their own.

In observing students using *The Multicultural Workshop*, we have been pleased to see how much fun they have, how eager they are to read and write, and how quickly their command of English grows. They become more critical and focused in their thinking, more insightful and analytic about life around them, and more connective and integrative in their relationship to texts.

❖ **UNITS AND THEMES.** Each of five units of *The Multicultural Workshop: Book 3* is designed around a different theme. The themes—**choices, identity, change, conflict,** and **relationships**—are universal and time-less, allowing students to ask meaningful questions and explore issues that concern all of us as human beings. However, because we are all shaped by our particular cultures and life experiences, answers to the questions we ask and our articulation of the issues that concern us will differ from person to person.

The Multicultural Workshop: Book 3 directs students to approach these differences analytically and respectfully, building on the rich cultural environment of the classroom to promote and develop critical thinking skills—and the strategies needed by students to explore their differences (and similarities) through reading and writing. Field testing has shown us that the themes work well in providing a context for limited-English students to draw from their varied backgrounds—to discuss and read and write about what they know—without intrusion into their private lives.

❖ **CHAPTERS AND THEMES.** Each unit comprises four chapters, designed around a different aspect of the unit theme. For example, Chapter One in Unit Two—the unit on **identity**—focuses on how we learn our gender roles; Chapter Two explores the ties between gender identity and body language; Chapter Three examines what can happen when gender roles conflict across cultures; and Chapter Four turns an analytic eye to the effects of gender stereotyping. The close thematic tie among the chapters of a unit makes it possible for students to work 'across' texts, as they will be expected to do in the academic mainstream.

❖ **FINAL PROJECT OF EACH UNIT.** Each unit ends with a summative writing activity, called the "final project." From their writing folders, students select one draft for further work from among the pieces of writing drafted during the course of the unit. Supported by reflections on the writing process and notes on revising, students rework this piece of writing as the culminating activity of the four-chapter cycle. In the process, they begin to integrate the complex act of revising into their writing behavior.

❖ **ACTIVITIES.** The activities built into each unit are varied. Some activities direct students to work alone, in pairs, or in small groups; other activities involve the whole class, working together. Some activities call for journal work or drafting essays; others direct students to solve problems, analyze written texts, or relate information. Across activities, students are listening, speaking, reading, and writing.

Some activities requiring writing can be completed in space provided in the textbook; some can best be completed on the board; others require students to use their own notebook paper. In addition to the textbook, each student needs a separate notebook to serve as a journal, a manila folder or accordion file to serve as a writing folder, and a supply of notebook paper.

❖ **REFERENCE GUIDE.** At the back of *The Multicultural Workshop: Book 3* is a guide, keyed to the reading, writing, and critical thinking strategies highlighted in small boxes in the margins of the chapters. The guide explains each strategy, gives examples and illustrations, and defines terms. Overall, the reference guide provides significant information that student writers need to know, not only to complete the tasks in the book but to understand what proficient academic readers and writers do.

For example, the first task in the first chapter of Unit One directs students to interpret the title of a newspaper article. The small box in the margin instructs students wanting to know more about interpreting to turn to page 262 of the reference guide. On that page, students can learn what interpreting is, how it works, and what purpose it serves. The reference guide serves as a handy tool, and it allows the body of the textbook to remain uncluttered and free of the instructional apparatus that can get in students' way.

How Does the Program Work in the Classroom?

❖ **WORKSHOP APPROACH.** The classroom, as a workshop, becomes a busy place. At times, students may all be talking at once, as they work in pairs or small groups. Students may be working on different tasks at the same time. Overall, more energy is expended, more talking goes on, and more action takes place in a workshop classroom.

In our field testing, we have also heard a lot of laughter and observed faces intent on listening to what their classmates had to say. We were impressed by students' respect for each other's opinions and by their willingness to work together. In our field testing, we also found the workshop approach to work well across cultures, with both males and females and within a considerable range of ages.

The workshop approach is based on the theoretical tenets of collaborative learning and on language acquisition theory, both supporting the notion that students learn in general—and learn to read, speak, and write a language, in particular—through interacting with others in meaningful ways. A learner's intent to communicate must drive each interaction; otherwise, little learning takes place. Meaningful communication requires interaction: hence, the workshop classroom, with its collaborative tasks, shared writing, discussions, and reader-response groups.

❖ **ORIENTATION FOR STUDENTS.** The workshop approach may be new to ESL students. Students may enter class with the point of view that every scrap of writing must not only be read but corrected by the teacher; that they can learn only from the teacher, the figure of authority; and that their classmates, whose English is not perfect, have nothing to offer them.

We urge you to explain to students that workshop methodology is theoretically sound; that they will get far more practice in groups and pairs than if class time is divided by the number of students enrolled; that the materials have been successfully tested on students just like them; and that a new approach is always awkward at first. Ultimately, you may need to ask them to give the approach a chance, based on the philosophy of "Try it. You'll like it."

To teachers who have never used a workshop approach in ESL classes, we offer the same philosophy. Keep in mind that it takes a while for both teachers and students to "get the hang" of a workshop. We urge you not to abandon certain kinds of activities that seem unsuccessful the first or second time you try them. For example, in the field testing we saw some students initially having difficulty with inferencing. However, after the teacher modeled the activity, gave examples, and "talked" students through the process, they had no more trouble with it. Let students know that it is normal to have difficulty with something that is new—and then carry on.

❖ **GROUP WORK.** We offer the following tips on group work:

· Groups of 3–4 seem to work best.

· Mix languages; this establishes English as a valid "lingua franca."

· Mix strengths and weaknesses.

· To get the mixes indicated above, you may need to be the one dividing up the class. However, if the mixes are not a problem, students can count off or choose their own groups.

· With group work requiring continuity, keep the same groupings; change groupings when students begin a new cycle of work.

· Insist on "good neighbor" rules within groups: respect everyone's contribution; encourage everyone to participate and to give feedback to each other.

· Circulate during group work. When you hear or see something praiseworthy, point it out. Students learn the dynamics of positive group work in this way.

Reading in The Multicultural Workshop: Book 3

❖ **VARIED GENRES.** Readings in each unit relate to the unit theme and were selected for their potential interest to culturally-diverse groups of students. They are representative of a number of different genres: poems and short stories, newspaper and magazine articles, autobiographical and expository essays, and textbook excerpts. ESL students at the intermediate/low-advanced level need to strengthen their base of critical literacy across a number of genres before concentrating on the kinds of academic texts they will be required to manage—in volume— in their mainstream courses. *The Multicultural Workshop: Book 3* eases students into critical literacy and academic texts.

❖ **READING COMPREHENSION.** The readings in *Book 3* provide contexts within which students interact; they do not serve as models for student writing, although we fully expect students to internalize aspects of the language of the readings as they work their way through the textbook.

Following a reading, various activities prompt students to tie in their own knowledge, experience, and opinions—as all proficient readers do—in order to build a framework for comprehending a reading. Students are also called on to bring these connections into their writing, as they begin to analyze their own views and experience against others' perceptions of related experience.

❖ **READING STRATEGIES.** In our experience, some students comprehend little when they read because, in part, they have developed few strategies for creating comprehension for themselves. A great deal of the focus in *Book 3* is on helping students develop and use these strategies, among which are the following:

- predicting
- paraphrasing
- scanning
- taking notes

- summarizing
- finding main ideas
- asking questions
- inferencing

A complete listing of strategies built into and practiced in *The Multicultural Workshop: Book 3* can be found on pages 249–257.

❖ **APPROACH TO READINGS.** At first glance, the readings in each unit appear more difficult than one might expect intermediate/low-advanced ESL students to be able to handle. Our field testing shows that these readings are not out of students' reach so long as the tasks we ask them to perform on the texts are sensible and realisitic. In previewing the readings in *Book 3,* keep in mind that we are asking students to **respond** to the readings not "learn" them.

❖ **USING THE RESOURCE BOX.** The resource box provides a number of benefits to students: it allows for reading experience additional to the textbook; it motivates students by providing a choice of readings and a sense of self-directed progress; and it offers activities that reinforce and expand strategies used in the textbook.

Teachers and students can use the readings in the resource box in a number of ways. For a class that meets three days a week or more, one class period each week can be designated "free reading day," with students choosing their readings and working independently from the box. For programs that have a separate reading laboratory, students may be encouraged or required to do work from the box outside of class and on their own time.

Writing in The Multicultural Workshop: Book 3

❖ **WRITERS' NEEDS.** The writing activities are based on our convictions about the needs of ESL students preparing to enter the academic mainstream. Some of these needs relate to the kinds of texts students produce; others, to the way they go about producing them. As we see it, student writers at this level of proficiency need the following:

• to gain greater fluency in writing

• to strengthen their individual voices

• to plumb their individual reservoirs of knowledge and experience—and articulate what they know

• to tie their knowledge and experience to the knowledge and experience of others

• to increase their awareness of writing as a process, with revising as a central aspect of that process

• to apply strategies to enhance the process

• to "layer" their writing through evaluating, interpreting, etc. in order to provide a writer's perspective on the topic; in other words, to examine and not simply report

• to have fun and achieve enough success to keep working at the hard job of writing better.

The writing activities in *Book 3* are designed to meet these needs without overwhelming or intimidating students. By design, the writing activities do not look like traditional academic tasks, yet they engage students in the sophisticated strategies needed for academic work.

❖ **WRITING JOURNALS.** Throughout *Book 3,* students are directed to make entries in their writing journals. The entries should be dated. The journal may be, in actuality, a spiral notebook; in any case, it should be separate from other notebooks in which students take class notes or write their assignments.

Students are encouraged to use their journals to collect ideas and information for their writing, to experiment, and to explore ideas they may want to pursue later. Basically, a journal is a writer's storehouse.

We strongly urge that you not correct or grade journal entries. If you collect and read students' journals, we encourage you to respond as a reader. You might enter a comment such as "I like this idea!" or "I know what you mean," where appropriate. You might refer to your own ideas and experience, with a comment such as "The same thing happened to me." In our experience, students seem more committed to keeping a journal if they know they will have a reader. Overall, though, the basic point is this: every writer needs to keep a journal, whether it is read by someone else or not.

❖ **WRITING FOLDERS.** At the end of each chapter, students complete a writing task, which they then place in their writing folders. The writing task relates to the work of the chapter and directions for it are given, although students always have latitude as to what they actually write. Each writer has to be free to come up with what she/he wants to say; otherwise, the writing is sterile and meaningless. If students interpret the directions differently and veer in different directions in completing the assignment, that should be no problem.

The writing completed at the end of each chapter becomes a first draft in the writing folder. It should be dated and numbered by the unit and chapter of the textbook—for example, "September 15, 1995, Unit One, Chapter Two, Draft 1." By the end of each unit, then, writers have completed four first drafts. Whether or not a draft gets more work depends on the writer's interest.

To complete the final project of each unit, students choose one of their first drafts from their writing folder for further work. Urge them to choose one that really interests them, one they are willing to put more effort and energy into. It may not be the draft you would choose, but the choice should be left to the individual writer.

It is while working on their final project for the unit that students learn the lessons all writers must learn: revising is plain hard work. It may take three, four, five (+) drafts for a writer to work out what he/she wants to say; and with each draft, the writer discovers more about the topic of the writing.

❖ **FEEDBACK.** We recommend that you meet with students in individual conferences during the multiple-drafting period to give them feedback and direction for further revising. In any case, you need to find the means and time to comment on students' efforts leading to the last draft of a writing cycle. Student writers want to know what they are doing well and where they need to improve. Overall, though, we encourage you to focus on effort and improvement. It is not realistic to expect perfection from intermediate/low-advanced ESL writers, and unreasonably high standards for grammatical accuracy can stifle a developing writer, in our experience.

It is important to remember that ESL students at this level of proficiency are **in the process of becoming** good writers, readers, and speakers of English; they are not there yet. The process is developmental and incremental, and it requires constant internal adjustment and readjustment on the learner's part. And, as ESL teachers know, it requires patience, faith, good will, and a long-range perspective on the teacher's part.

Students' last drafts in each writing cycle can be collected and placed in a special booklet—a binder or folder—for everyone in the class to read. Sharing writing provides a crucial benefit to writers, especially developing writers: it establishes a sense of community, a bond, that works in subtle ways to promote better writing. The booklet could be a group booklet, containing the writing of the whole class, or a separate booklet for each student. After being circulated, the drafts can be returned to the writing folders of their rightful owners, unless copies can be made.

❖ **SUMMARY: JOURNAL AND WRITING FOLDER.** For easy access, here is a summary of key points about the writing folder and journal:

- Each student needs a special notebook to serve as a writing journal.

- As students work through each chapter of the textbook, they are directed to write in their journals, although they can also be encouraged to make entries on their own.

- Writers use journals to store ideas and information and to experiment with putting them into writing.

- Students' journals should not be corrected or graded; the teacher should respond as a reader to students' entries.

- Journal entries should be dated.

- Each student needs a manila folder or accordion file to serve as a writing folder.

- At the end of each chapter, a piece of writing goes into the writing folder as a first draft.

- At the end of each fourth chapter, students choose one of their first drafts and revise it until they can do no more with it. This constitutes the "final project" of a unit.

- All drafts in the writing folder should be dated and numbered.

- Individual student conferences are essential during the revising process, while students are completing their final projects.

- Teacher evaluation of students' writing should focus on effort and improvement.

Student Evaluation

❖ **EVALUATING THE WRITING FOLDER.** Students using *The Multicultural Workshop: Book 3* can be best evaluated at the end of the semester on the basis of their writing folders. Here, the evaluator needs to view a student's work across the whole academic term—from first to last entry in the folder—and also to analyze a student's process of revising across the drafts of a multi-draft piece of writing, particularly one completed at the end of the term.

❖ **EVALUATING WRITING.** While an increasing control over sentence-level grammar is important, other aspects of students' writing are of equal importance. We urge you to keep the following questions in mind when evaluating a student's writing:

- Has the writer begun to develop a distinct voice?

- Does the writer reach beyond simply reporting events to examining their importance in the overall context of the topic?

- Does the writer know how to establish a limited focus?

- Does the writer show an increasing awareness of an audience by explaining, illustrating, giving examples, or in some way amplifying important points?

- Does the writer use clear language?

- Does the writer attempt to make her/his writing interesting? Are details vivid? Are examples relevant?

- Can a reader follow the writer's thinking and arrangement of ideas?

- Has the writer begun to develop a clear sense of introduction, body, and conclusion, where appropriate?

- Does the writer show a sense of being able to make positive changes in any of the aspects above over the course of several drafts? In other words, is the writer beginning to revise his/her writing?

Intermediate/low-advanced students will not be perfect writers by the end of the term using any materials, but improvements in the areas indicated above are to be applauded and rewarded—and students will want to know where they are improving.

❖ **EVALUATING READING.** If the classroom teacher is expected to evaluate students' reading proficiency, we suggest the following: 1) select two or three reading cards for each student from the resource box, choosing from the section of the box that you and your colleagues think represents the level of difficulty your students should be capable of reading; 2) Ask the student to choose whichever card she/he likes best, read it, and write to a classmate, telling enough about the reading to interest the classmate and explaining why the reader thinks the classmate might want to read it; 3) Then collect students' writing, keeping a student's "review" together with the particular reading.

As you read a student's "review," keep these questions in mind:

- Does the reader show that she/he is able to follow the reading?

- Does the reader synthesize enough of the reading to be able to tell someone else about it?

- Does the reader show evidence of discerning certain aspects of the reading that might interest another reader?

- Does the reader bring his/her own views to bear on the reading? Does the reader use those views to make sense of the reading?

- Does the reader relate any aspect of the reading to other readings?

If you discern some of these complexities in students' responses to readings, then your students are on their way to becoming proficient readers.

❖ **OTHER EVALUATION SCENARIOS.** End-of-term evaluation procedures vary greatly from program to program, so the scenario detailed above—with the classroom teacher evaluating students' writing and/or reading—may not apply. While we think it ideal for students using *The Multicultural Workshop: Book 3* to be evaluated on the basis of their classwork, other scenarios are possible:

- In programs with portfolio assessment, the scenario is barely different from the one above for evaluating writing. Students' writing folders **are** their portfolios, and someone other than the classroom teacher will probably serve as evaluator.

- In programs with a proficiency examination determining course grades and future placement, a student's writing folder might be reviewed by an "appeals" committee in cases where the classroom teacher knows that the exam results do not give a true reading of that student's proficiency.

- In some programs, proficiency examination results might be combined with a student's course work—for workshop students, the writing and/or reading evaluation detailed above—to determine the course grade and future placement.

- In programs with competency-based assessment, the listing of reading, writing, and critical thinking strategies at the front of the book can help determine the match between the skills required by a program curriculum and those employed by workshop students. In this scenario, an examination might need to be constructed by teachers using the workshop materials to test to what degree of proficiency their students use the strategies.

Authors' Invitation

Teachers across the United States have provided input to the creation of *The Multicultural Workshop*—through the review process and field testing of the materials. Perhaps because we, ourselves, are ESL teachers, we feel that ESL teachers know best what works in the classroom and we have benefited greatly from other teachers' suggestions. If you have questions about the materials or, after using them, have feedback that you would be willing to pass along to us, we would be happy to hear from you via Heinle & Heinle.

The Multicultural Workshop provides a collection of readings (essays, short stories, poems, newspaper and magazine articles, and excerpts from books) as well as writing and discussion activities. Each of the readings and activities relates to one of five themes:

• Identity

• Change

• Choices

• Relationships

• Conflict

Your journal is your personal notebook. You can list ideas, take notes, draw, or do whatever you want in your journal. Your journal writing will not be corrected.

What You Will Be Doing in The Multicultural Workshop

Throughout the program you will be reading, writing, and discussing ideas with your classmates.

Sometimes you will write your ideas in your journal.

Sometimes you will discuss ideas with a partner or with a group of classmates.

In each unit you will also complete four writing assignments. These pieces of writing will go into your writing folder. At the end of each unit, you will select one paper to revise. (You will learn more about the revision process at the end of each unit.) Your teacher will use your revised writing to help you evaluate your progress.

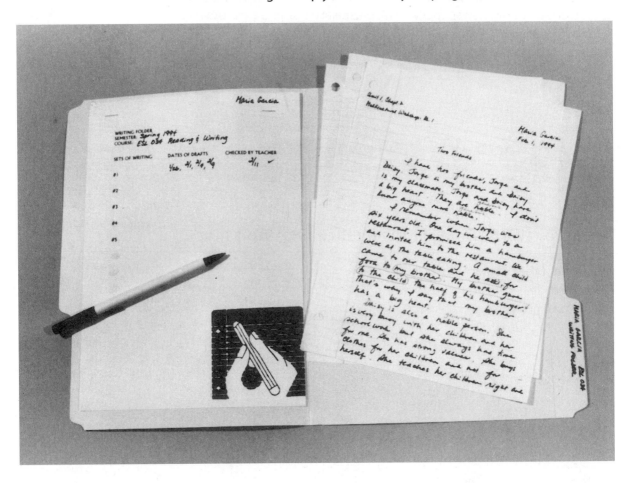

On pages 237–263, you will find a Reference Guide. This section identifies some of the strategies you can use to improve your reading and writing.

THE MULTICULTURAL WORKSHOP

BOOK 3

UNIT ONE
Career Choices

In this unit you will read four selections related to the theme of career choices.

- Which of the occupations shown here is interesting to you? Why?
- What kinds of things do these people do at work?
- What kinds of training do these people need for their jobs?

CHAPTER ONE

Choosing a Career

CRITICAL THINKING STRATEGY:
Interpreting
See page 262.

1. Class Work. What does the title of the newspaper article on pages 5–7 mean to you? Based on the title, what do you think the article is about?

WRITING STRATEGY:
Making a Tree Diagram
See page 244.

2. Class Work. In your opinion, what does it take to be a successful scientist? List your ideas in a tree diagram on the board.

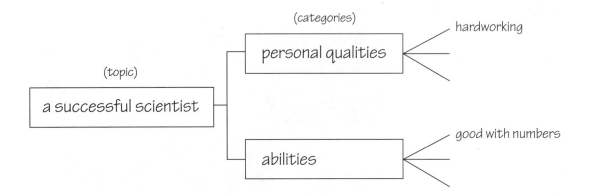

(topic)

a successful scientist

(categories)

personal qualities → hardworking

abilities → good with numbers

READING STRATEGY:
Reading for Specific Information
See page 254.

3. On your own. As you read the article on pages 5–7, underline the words and phrases that describe a successful scientist.

So-So[1] Student, Nobel Prize-Winner

by Rushworth M. Kidder

from *The Christian Science Monitor*

1   As particle physicist Leon M. Lederman remembers it, he wasn't naturally good with his hands. As a youngster growing up in the Depression years[2] in New York City, he wasn't all that curious about how things worked. He wasn't a very good student. He found math difficult. His first year as a graduate student in physics at Columbia University was terrible. So he applied to transfer to the Massachusetts Institute of Technology—and was refused.

2   And then, in 1988, he shared the Nobel Prize in physics for his 1962 discovery of a second neutrino, an elementary subatomic particle.

3   What got him launched and kept him going? In an interview in his office at the Fermi National Accelerator Laboratory, which he directed from 1979 until 1989, he points to the people who spurred him on.[3]

4   Two things happened, he recalls, when he was 10 years old. First, one day when he was sick in bed, his father brought him a book co-authored by Albert Einstein about relativity. "It started out comparing physics to a detective story," he says, "and it was in big print. That's very important at ten years old."

5   "The other thing was a front-page article in *The New York Times* about the winning of the Nobel Prize by Carl Anderson for discovering the positron. It told how he took a cloud chamber to the top of a mountain. And that was the most romantic thing I could think of—to drag some instrument up there and see something."

6   Later, during high school, Lederman began hanging around the chemistry lab with "three or four friends" after school. The lab assistant was "a lively guy who let us fool around and blow glass." It was these friendships, more than any conceptual[4] fascination, that kept his interest in science alive.

7   But it wasn't until graduate school—after finishing City College and spending three years in the Army—that he finally developed self-confidence as a budding[5] scientist.

8   One day, he says, he came back to the laboratory after spending a few

---

1 **so-so**   neither good nor bad; mediocre
2 **Depression years**   the 1930s, a period of terrible economic hardship
3 **spurred him on**   encouraged him
4 **conceptual**   about ideas
5 **budding**   beginning to develop

months studying for his qualifying exams, and "there was a guy mopping the floor and singing in Italian, and I said, 'Oh, a new janitor.' And as I came in he said something incomprehensible, and I said, 'Yeah, but watch out for those wires—don't get 'em wet.'"

As it happened, the man was a visiting physics professor from Rome— part of the flood of scientists fleeing postwar Europe. Having just arrived, he was given directions to the lab, found it was dirty, and began cleaning it up. "He was doing research in cosmic rays. And he was the first one who made me think that maybe I was not all that dumb."

So if an innate[6] gift for science is not essential, what are the qualities that make a scientist?

The first, says Lederman, is "total dedication." Scientists need "resistance to being discouraged," he says. "You've got to be able to live through the low periods, of which there are many. You need a willingness to work hard and be single-minded—think about what you're doing while you're shaving. It's got to be able to obsess you completely, so that you're not interested in vacations or sleeping or eating or anything. Naturally at some point you've got to lift your head up. But you need to be able to go for three months or so with naps on cots and whatever food comes out of the coin machine."

Equally important, says Lederman, is imagination. "A lot of people are tremendously insightful—they have mathematical abilities, they have analytical abilities. They're super students. But there must be something else, because I don't have any of those, and I'm successful."

By imagination, he says, he means the ability to say, "look, there are 500 bright guys looking at the same problem you're looking at. Since it's still a problem, not one of those guys has gotten it. Therefore this problem must have some side to it that none of those 500 guys has seen. What could it be? I know we're going to solve this problem within the next ten years, so why can't I do it tonight?"

"I think it's not only the ability but almost the preference for thinking unconventionally[7]—and trying hard to identify with the little kid who said the emperor has no clothes."[8]

In addition, Lederman feels it's important for today's scientist to be "a people person." In the kind of experiments conducted at Fermilab, "you need these large collaborations[9]—and it's helpful if you're a social person. You get more out of it."

6 **innate**   born with
7 **unconventionally**   in unusual ways
8 **the little kid who said the emperor has no clothes**   a character in a folktale who was the only one to see the truth
9 **collaborations**   work done by two or more people working together

Leon Lederman

16   That sort of sociability also helps broaden scientists beyond their basic field—an important part of modern science. "You need to keep in touch with many of the contiguous[10] fields," he says, "because you never know when a good idea will come out that you can apply."

17   According to Lederman, the thrill of scientific discovery is still part of his experience. "When you know something that you're the only one to know—and there are 4 or 5 billion people on the planet, and it's so profound that it will affect all of their lives at some point—that's something science can do. And there's nothing else I know of that can do that."

---

10 **contiguous**   related

READING STRATEGY:
Using Context
See page 255.

4. On your own. Use context—the words and ideas around an unfamiliar word—to guess the meaning of the underlined words below. Then look up each word in a dictionary and choose the meaning that best fits the word in this context.

a. "What got him launched and kept him going?"

My guess: _____

Dictionary definition: _____

b. "…he [Anderson] took a cloud chamber to the top of a mountain. And that was the most romantic thing I could think of—to drag some instrument up there and see something."

My guess: _____

Dictionary definition: _____

c. "One day, he [Lederman] says, he came back to the laboratory after spending a few months studying for his qualifying exams, and there was a guy mopping the floor and singing in Italian, and I said, 'Oh, a new janitor.'"

My guess: _____

Dictionary definition: _____

d. "It [your work] has got to be able to obsess you completely, so that you're not interested in vacations or sleeping or eating or anything."

My guess: _____

Dictionary definition: _____

e. "When you know something that you're the only one to know—and there are 4 or 5 billion people on the planet, and it's so underline{profound} that it will affect all of their lives at some point—that's something science can do."

My guess: _____

Dictionary definition: _____

Compare ideas with your classmates.

5. **Pair Work.** What inferences can you make based on the information in the sentences below?

⬙⦿⬙⬙⦿⬙⬙⦿⬙⬙⦿⬙
READING STRATEGY:
Making Inferences
See page 252.

a. "Two things happened, he [Lederman] recalls, when he was 10 years old. First, one day when he was sick in bed, his father brought him a book co-authored by Albert Einstein about relativity."

What can you infer about Lederman's father?

_____

b. According to Lederman, another thing that influenced him to become a scientist was "a front-page article in the *New York Times* about the winning of the Nobel Prize by Carl Anderson for discovering the positron. It told how he took a cloud chamber to the top of a mountain. And that was the most romantic thing I could think of—to drag some instrument up there and see something."

What inference can you make about Lederman?

_____

c. "..., during high school, Lederman began hanging around the chemistry lab with 'three or four friends' after school. The lab assistant was 'a lively guy who let us fool around and blow glass.'"

What can you infer about the lab assistant?

_____

d. "..., the man was a visiting physics professor from Rome—part of the flood of scientists fleeing postwar Europe. Having just arrived, he was given directions to the lab, found it was dirty, and began cleaning it up."

What can you infer about the visiting physics professor?

_____

Share ideas with your classmates.

<table>
<tr><td>

⬛⬛◇⬛⬛◇⬛⬛◇⬛⬛◇⬛

WRITING STRATEGY:
Using Quotations
See page 248.

</td></tr>
</table>

6. **On your own.** According to Leon Lederman, what are the qualities that make a scientist successful? Look back at the words and phrases in the article that you underlined. Then list these qualities, using quotations from the article.

Example:

According to Leon Lederman, one important quality that makes a scientist is "total dedication."

_____

_____

_____

_____

_____

_____

_____

_____

_____

_____

Compare ideas with your classmates.

7. **On your own.** Choose one of Lederman's statements from the article. As you think about this statement, write your ideas in your journal. Keep these ideas in mind as you write:

CRITICAL THINKING STRATEGY: *Analyzing* See page 258.

   • Use journal assignments to explore your own ideas.

   • There are no right or wrong answers in journal assignments.

   • Your journal writing will not be corrected.

   Example:

   > *In this article, Lederman says that a scientist has to be able to "live through the low periods, of which there are many." This must be especially true for a scientist because it might take many years of work to prove or discover something. There must be times when you feel like you are going nowhere, that your work is useless. If you can't live through the low periods, you are likely to give up easily. But this is true in many professions. All jobs have low periods, times when you feel like your work is not very worthwhile… .*

   Get together with a partner. Identify the statement you wrote about and tell your partner about an idea from your journal writing.

8. **Group Work.** Look at the reading on pages 5–7 with a writer's eye. As you discuss each question below, take turns recording your group's ideas.

CRITICAL THINKING STRATEGY: *Analyzing* See page 258.

   a. Do you think the introduction is effective? Why or why not?

   b. The topic of this article is Leon Lederman. How did the writer focus the topic? In other words, what specific questions about Lederman did he answer?

   c. In your opinion, what is the writer trying to accomplish in this article?

   d. Which details create the most vivid image for you? Describe what you "see."

   Use your notes to report your group's ideas to the class.

READING STRATEGY:
Summarizing
See page 254.

9. **Group Work.** A summary is a restatement of the most important ideas in an article. It is shorter and easier to understand than the original article. Read this sample summary of the article on pages 5–7 and answer the questions that follow.

> R. M. Kidder's article about Leon Lederman, a Nobel prize-winning physicist, demonstrates two basic things: 1) personal success is built on self-confidence and 2) self-confidence develops from positive relationships with friends and colleagues. From Kidder's brief story of Lederman's life, we learn that Lederman, as a youngster, was not at all curious about how things worked. He was not a good student, and he found math difficult. Later, however, after positive encounters with people interested in physics, he realized he was not dumb. He began to use his imagination for the first time and to suggest ideas that no one had thought of before. According to Kidder, Lederman credits dedication, imagination, and sociability for his success as a scientist. Above all, though, he had to believe that he could <u>be</u> a scientist.

a. What important information does the writer of the summary include at the beginning?

b. Does this summary include the important ideas that you underlined (Activity 3)?

c. Does the writer include any unnecessary details?

d. Is the summary easier to understand than the original article?

Report your group's ideas to the class.

WRITING STRATEGY:
Brainstorming
See page 237.

WRITING STRATEGY:
Collecting Information
See page 238.

10. **Writing Project.** Choose a career of interest to you. What does it take to be successful in this career? In writing, present your ideas to your classmates. Here are some suggestions to help you get started:

a. With several classmates, brainstorm a list of careers. Then choose one that interests you.

b. What does a person in this career do on the job? List what you already know. If possible, talk to someone with this career and collect more ideas. Then look for information about this career in your library. Take notes on what you find out.

c. What personal qualities and abilities does a person in this career need to have? To answer this question, think about the types of things this person does on the job. Then collect your ideas on a tree diagram.

WRITING STRATEGY:
*Making a
Tree Diagram*
See page 244.

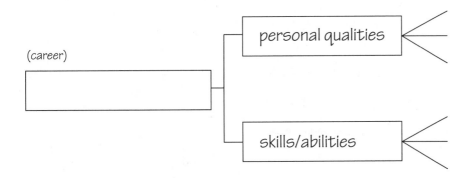

d. Explain your ideas to a classmate. Take notes on your classmate's suggestions and questions.

e. Look over your notes and choose the information you want to include in your writing. Think about how you might organize this information. What might your readers want to know first? What then?

WRITING STRATEGY:
Organizing Ideas
See page 245.

f. Write a first draft of your paper.

g. Exchange papers with a partner. Ask your partner to write down any questions he or she has.

h. Place a copy of your paper and your partner's questions in your writing folder.

CHAPTER TWO

Choosing Where to Work

WRITING STRATEGY:
Making a
Cluster Diagram
See page 241.

1. **Group Work.** What are the characteristics of a good employer? Together brainstorm a set of ideas. Take turns writing your group's ideas on a cluster diagram like this:

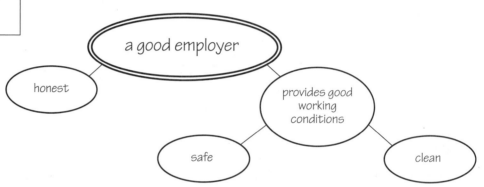

Look over your group's cluster diagram and together choose the three most important characteristics. Then tell your classmates which characteristics you chose.

Would you like to work here?

2. **Group Work.** Read the title of the article on page 16 and the first paragraph. What reasons might the writer give to explain why he quit the company? Work together to list several possible reasons.

READING STRATEGY:
Predicting
See page 253.

_____

_____

_____

_____

_____

_____

_____

_____

Read your group's ideas to the class.

3. **On your own.** For one minute, scan the article on pages 16–18, looking specifically for the reasons why the writer, Tomoyuki Iwashita, quit the company. Underline any reasons you find. Then look back at your list of possible reasons in Activity 2. Which of Iwashita's reasons appear on your list? Tell your classmates.

READING STRATEGY:
Scanning
See page 254.

4. **On your own.** Writing down your thoughts and questions as you read can help you read actively. On pages 16–17, you can see what one reader wrote down as she read the first four paragraphs of the article. As you read the article, try writing your thoughts and questions in the margin.

READING STRATEGY:
Writing Margin Notes
See page 257.

Why I Quit the Company

by Tomoyuki Iwashita

from *The New Internationalist*

When I tell people that I quit working for the company after only a year, most of them think I'm crazy. They can't understand why I would want to give up a prestigious[1] and secure job. But I think I'd have been crazy to stay, and I'll try to explain why.

I started working for the company immediately after graduating from university. It's a big, well-known trading company with about 6,000 employees all over the world. There's a lot of competition to get into this and other similar companies, which promise young people a wealthy and successful future. I was set on course to be a Japanese "yuppie."[2]

I'd been used to living independently as a student, looking after myself and organizing my own schedule. As soon as I started working all that changed. I was given a room in the company dormitory, which is like a fancy hotel, with a twenty-four-hour hot bath service and all meals laid on. Most single company employees live in a dormitory like this, and many married employees live in company apartments. The dorm system is actually a great help because living in Tokyo costs more than young people earn—but I found it stifling.[3]

My life rapidly became reduced to a shuttle between the dorm and the office. The working day is officially eight hours, but you can never leave the office on time. I used to work from nine in the morning until eight or nine at night, and often until midnight. Drinking with colleagues after work is part of the job; you can't say no. The company building contained cafeterias, shops, a bank, a post office, a doctor's office, a barber's...I never needed to leave the building. Working, drinking, sleeping, and standing on a horribly crowded commuter train for an hour and a half each way: This was my life. I spent all my time with the same colleagues; when I wasn't involved in enter-

1 **prestigious**   highly respected
2 **yuppie**   young person who is advancing quickly
3 **stifling**   restrictive, limiting

taining clients on the weekend, I was expected to play golf with my colleagues. I soon lost sight of the world outside the company.

5   Overtiredness and overwork leave you little energy to analyze or criticize your situation. There are shops full of "health drinks," cocktails of caffeine and other drugs, which will keep you going even when you're exhausted. *Karoshi* (death from overwork) is increasingly common and is always being discussed in the newspapers. I myself collapsed from working too hard. My boss told me: "You should control your health; it's your own fault if you get sick." There is no paid sick leave;[4] I used up half of my fourteen days' annual leave[5] because of sickness.

6   The company also controls its employees' private lives. Many company employees under thirty are single. They are expected to devote all their time to the company and become good workers; they don't have time to find a girlfriend. The company offers scholarships to the most promising young employees to enable them to study abroad for a year or two. But unmarried people who are on these courses are not allowed to get married until they have completed the course! Married employees who are sent to train abroad have to leave their families in Japan for the first year.

7   In fact, the quality of married life is often determined by the husband's work. Men who have just gotten married try to go home early for a while, but soon have to revert to the norm[6] of late-night work. They have little time to spend with their wives and even on the weekend are expected to play golf with colleagues. Fathers cannot find time to communicate with their children and child rearing is largely left to mothers. Married men posted abroad will often leave their family behind in Japan; they fear that their children will fall behind in the fiercely competitive Japanese education system.

8   However, there are some signs that things are changing. Although many new employees in my company were quickly brainwashed,[7] many others, like myself, complained about life in the company and seriously considered leaving. But most of them were already in fetters—of debt. Pleased with themselves for getting into the company and anticipating a life of executive luxury, these new employees throw their money around.[8] Every night they are out drinking. They buy smart clothes and take a taxi back to the dormitory after the last train

Lost sight of world outside of work.

---

4 **sick leave**   time off from work because of illness
5 **annual leave**   vacation days allowed each year
6 **norm**   expected behavior
7 **brainwashed**   convinced; persuaded to believe something
8 **throw their money around**   spend their money quickly

has gone. They start borrowing money from the bank and soon they have a debt growing like a snowball rolling down a slope. The banks demand no security for loans; it's enough to be working for a well-known company. Some borrow as much as a year's salary in the first few months. They can't leave the company while they have such debts to pay off.

I was one of the few people in my intake of employees who didn't 9 get into debt. I left the company dormitory after three months to share an apartment with a friend. I left the company exactly one year after I entered it. It took me a while to find a new job, but I'm working as a journalist now. My life is still busy, but it's a lot better than it was. I'm lucky because nearly all big Japanese companies are like the one I worked for, and conditions in many small companies are even worse.

It's not easy to opt out of[9] a life-style that is generally considered to 10 be prestigious and desirable, but more and more young people in Japan are thinking about doing it. You have to give up a lot of superficially attractive material benefits in order to preserve the quality of your life and your sanity. I don't think I was crazy to leave the company. I think I would have gone crazy if I'd stayed.

---

9 **opt out of**   choose to leave

5. **Pair Work.** Work together to answer the questions below. Take notes on your discussion.

   a. Which of Iwashita's reasons for quitting makes the most sense to you? Why?

   b. Leon Lederman, the scientist described in chapter one, works very long hours, but he doesn't seem to mind. Iwashita, on the other hand, does not want to be totally dedicated to his company. How might you explain this difference?

   Share ideas from your discussion with your classmates.

> CRITICAL THINKING STRATEGY: *Evaluating* See page 261.
>
> *Comparing* See page 260.

6. **On your own.** Iwashita describes the trading company from the point of view of an unhappy employee. If the personnel managers were describing the company, what do you think they would say? In your journal, write a quick description of the company from the viewpoint of a personnel manager in the company Iwashita worked for.

> WRITING STRATEGY: *Using Point of View* See page 247.

7. **On your own.** Look back at the article to find the two-word verbs below. Use context to guess the meaning of each verb. Then write your own sentences using these verbs.

   a. Paragraph #2: *get into*

      My definition: _____

      New sentence: _____

   b. Paragraph #3: *look after*

      My definition: _____

      New sentence: _____

   c. Paragraph #5: *use up*

      My definition: _____

      New sentence: _____

d. Paragraph #8: *pay off*

My definition: _____

New sentence: _____

e. Paragraph #10: *give up*

My definition: _____

New sentence: _____

Read one of your sentences aloud to the class.

8. **On your own.** What would you like about working for the company described in the article? What wouldn't you like? Explore these questions as you write in your journal.

CRITICAL THINKING
STRATEGY:
Analyzing
See page 258.

9. **Group Work.** Look over the article with a writer's eye. As you discuss each question below, take turns recording your group's ideas.

a. How do you think this article would be different if it were written for a Japanese audience? What information might the writer add or delete?

b. What is Iwashita's purpose in writing this article? Where in the article does the writer's purpose become clear to you?

c. Do you think the writer provides enough details and examples to build a strong argument? Give an example.

d. Give your opinion of the introduction and the conclusion—excellent, good, fair, or poor—and explain why.

Take turns reporting your group's ideas to the class.

10. Writing Project. What would be the ideal place in which to work? In writing, describe this place to your classmates. Here are some suggestions to help you get started:

a. What would your ideal place to work be like? Try one or more of these strategies to collect ideas:

- Quickwrite for several minutes on the topic of the ideal place to work.

- Ask your friends about places where they worked. Find out what they liked and disliked.

- With a partner, brainstorm words and phrases that describe a good place to work.

b. Think of an interesting way to present your ideas to your classmates. For example, you could:

- Describe your ideal place to work from the point of view of the company president or personnel manager.

- Describe the company from the point of view of a satisfied employee.

- Write a conversation between two employees at the company cafeteria.

- Analyze the reasons for working for a particular company from the viewpoint of a career counselor giving advice to a young person.

c. Write a first draft of your paper.

d. Place a copy of your writing in your writing folder.

WRITING STRATEGY: *Quickwriting* See page 246.
Collecting Information See page 238.
Brainstorming See page 237.
Using Point of View See page 247.

CHAPTER THREE

Making Difficult Career Decisions

WRITING STRATEGY:
Brainstorming
See page 237.

1. **Class Work.** What are some of the decisions that people have to make while pursuing a career? Together brainstorm a list of ideas.

   Example: when to retire

   Look over your list. Which of these decisions might be especially hard to make? Why?

READING STRATEGY:
Predicting
See page 253.

Previewing
See page 253.

2. **Class Work.** The passage on the next page is an excerpt from a longer essay. In this part of the essay, the writer explains that her father had to defer, or put aside, his plans for the future. Why might this be? Together brainstorm a set of possible reasons.

3. **Class Work.** Read the first paragraph of the passage on page 23 and then stop to think about what you have read. Here are some questions to discuss:

   a. From whose point of view is the passage written?

   b. What seems to be the writer's topic?

   c. What questions does this paragraph raise for you?

READING STRATEGY:
Writing Margin Notes
See page 257.

4. **On your own.** As you read the passage, underline the important ideas. You might also want to write your thoughts and questions in the margin.

The Hopeland

by K. Kam

from *Making Waves,* an anthology of writings by Asian-American women

1   As a young man, my father lived in Hong Kong. He had worked hard to come to America, taking English classes at night to improve his timid, halting speech. He postponed marriage until he was thirty-one, reluctant to take a wife when he might leave for America the following year. But after a decade of pursuing his dream, he decided to marry my mother in 1959. Three years later, America opened her arms to my father, willing to embrace him after years of snubbing.[1] My mother, less eager, stood defenseless against the powerful charms of America.

2   My father rarely speaks any more of his deferred dreams. But I have plowed restless fingers through his bookshelves and stumbled upon Shakespeare readers tucked between the Chinese novels with their musty trunk[2] smells, and then a series of English grammar texts, old and yellowed with blotches of tea stains on the pages. I've raided his bookshelves section by section and have found hidden delights each time—a Sinclair Lewis novel, a Tennessee Williams play, a book of poetry. It was impossible for me to imagine my father's thickly accented syllables wrapping themselves around the elegant words.

3   When he first came to this country, his dreams incubated in the heat of a stuffy kitchen by day and pecked a little further out of their confining shells at night. Hard shells—language barriers, uncertainties, prejudices, fears—were chipped away bit by bit as he attended night school and struggled to become an educated man, a new success in a new land. Week after week, he sat

---

1 **snubbing**   treating rudely by ignoring
2 **trunk**   large box to carry one's belongings

under the glaring fluorescent lights of the classroom eking[3] out gram-ma-ti-cal essays as English teachers with pleased smiles and small nods of approval assigned him book after book of "American reading."

But somewhere far in the past, my father stopped the weary 4 tasks of "American reading" and writing assigned essays. He relegated[4] his American books to the shelves and focused his energy upon the persistent questioning of his children, each of whom had gone off to college.

"What are you going to do next year when you graduate?" 5

"I'm not sure yet, Dad. I'm thinking of working for a couple 6 of years, and then maybe I'll go back to school," answers his son, the one who studied economics.

"Why don't you become a dentist?" my father urges. 7

"It's not that easy, Dad. Besides, I don't want to become a dentist." 8

Once, when I worked for a group of attorneys in San 9 Francisco, my father asked where all of them had attended law school. "Where do they go on vacations? Do they ski? Do they own houses up in the mountains?" I was reluctant to answer, not wanting to fan[5] age-old disappointments. Before I could reply, he sighed, "You know, a very nice doctor comes into the restaurant all the time, and he always seems sad to me. I ask him what is wrong and he tells me his son is no good—uses too many drugs. Sells them, too. He asks me what my kids do and I tell him four are college graduates. He says that's beautiful, says I'm a lucky man."

His words startled[6] me. When we had run home from grade 10 school with near-perfect report cards, my father admonished us solemnly. "Never compare yourselves to those below you, only to those above you," he said year after year. My mother chided us, too. "You must study hard and make something of yourselves. When I was in China, I had to leave school at fourteen and start

---

3 **eking out** do something with difficulty
4 **relegated** put in a less important position
5 **fan** bring back; stir up
6 **startled** surprised; shocked

working as a seamstress in Hong Kong when I was sixteen. If I had been given the same opportunities you've received, I could have become anything I wanted—anything."

11   Their words seep into my blood and cause my muscles to pull taut.[7] At times I am frustrated by the pressure to succeed, yet I am driven by guilt and sadness to redress[8] my parents' lost dreams and regrets of an uneducated past.

---

7 **taut**   tight
8 **redress**   make up for; correct an injustice

5. On your own. Choose a word from the list to replace each under-lined word or phrase. Then rewrite each sentence, using the words that you chose. Compare sentences with a classmate.

a. "…I have <u>plowed</u> restless fingers through his bookshelves and <u>stumbled upon</u> Shakespeare readers <u>tucked</u> between the Chinese novels. …"

found	used	pushed
placed	written	touched

_____

_____

_____

b. "When he first came to this country, his dreams <u>incubated</u> in the heat of a stuffy kitchen by day and <u>pecked</u> a little further out of their confining shells at night."

grew	waited	moved
came true	lay	died

_____

_____

_____

READING STRATEGY:
Using Context
See page 255.

Read the sentences below and use context to come up with your own definition of each <u>underlined</u> word or phrase.

c. I had to <u>plow</u> through the reading assignment because I only had one hour to read 100 pages.

My definition: _____

d. While we were looking for a grocery store, we <u>stumbled upon</u> a great restaurant.

My definition: _____

e. He <u>tucked</u> a love letter into his wife's suitcase, knowing she would find it later.

My definition: _____

f. Between writing first and second drafts of a paper, I usually need to let my ideas <u>incubate</u>.

My definition: _____

g. I watched the chickens <u>pecking</u> the hard ground for small bits of corn left from the night before.

My definition: _____

Get together with a classmate and compare ideas.

6. **On your own.** What inferences can you make based on these sentences from the passage on page 23?

a. "As a young man, my father lived in Hong Kong. He had worked hard to come to America, taking English classes at night to improve his timid, halting speech."

What inferences can you make about the writer's father?

_____

_____

b. "My father rarely speaks any more of his deferred dreams. But I have plowed restless fingers through his bookshelves and stumbled upon Shakespeare readers tucked between the Chinese novels with their musty trunk smells, and then a series of English grammar texts, old and yellowed with blotches of tea stains on the pages."

What inferences can you make about the writer's father?

_____

_____

Compare ideas with your classmates.

> ▨▧◈▥▨▧◈▥▨▧◈▥▨◈
> **READING STRATEGY:**
> *Making Inferences*
> See page 252.

CRITICAL THINKING
STRATEGY:
Interpreting
See page 262.

7. **On your own.** Write your response to each of the quotations below. You might, for example, explain what the quotation tells you about the writer or her father. You might also tell what it makes you think of from your own experience.

a. "But somewhere far in the past, my father stopped the weary task of 'American reading' and writing assigned essays. He relegated his American books to the shelves and focused his energy upon the persistent questioning of his children, each of whom had gone off to college."

_____

_____

_____

_____

_____

_____

b. "When we had run home from grade school with near-perfect report cards, my father admonished us solemnly. 'Never compare yourselves to those below you, only to those above you,' he said year after year."

_____

_____

_____

_____

_____

_____

c. "At times I am frustrated by the pressure to succeed, yet I am driven by guilt and sadness to redress my parents' lost dreams and regrets of an uneducated past."

_____

_____

_____

_____

_____

_____

Get together with a partner and compare ideas.

8. **Group Work.** Choose one or more of these questions to discuss in your group. Ask one person to take notes on your group's discussion.

   a. What career opportunities did the writer's father have? What did he choose to do? Why?

   b. What conflict does the writer feel? What advice would you give her?

   c. Do you think the writer's father is proud of his children? Why or why not?

   d. Do you think the writer's father is a successful man? Why or why not?

Share your group's ideas with the class.

> **CRITICAL THINKING STRATEGY:**
> *Analyzing*
> See page 258.

9. **Group Work.** Look over the reading with a writer's eye. As you discuss the questions below, record your group's ideas.

   a. What do you think the writer's purpose is? Does the writer state her purpose?

   b. Which of the writer's words and phrases really help you to "see" her father? Give several examples.

   c. Is there anything else that you want to learn about the writer's father? What?

   d. What does the dialogue between the father and his children contribute?

> **CRITICAL THINKING STRATEGY:**
> *Analyzing*
> See page 258.

e. Which details do you find the most interesting? Why?

Share your group's ideas with the class.

CRITICAL THINKING
STRATEGY:
Synthesizing
See page 263.

10. **Class Work.** Choose three of your classmates to roleplay Leon Lederman, Tomoyuki Iwashita, and K. Kam. Invite these three guests to participate in a panel discussion on the topic of choosing careers. Together prepare a list of questions to ask your visitors. Then take turns asking your guests to answer your questions.

11. **Writing Project.** Choose the quotation below that interests you the most. Then in writing, tell your classmates what the quotation means to you. Use examples and details to explain your ideas. You can use the suggestions below to help you get started.

    "When work is a pleasure, life is a joy! When work is a duty, life is slavery."
    —*Maxim Gorky* (Russian novelist and playwright, 1868–1936)

    "Vocations which we wanted to pursue, but didn't, bleed, like colors, on the whole of our existence."
    —*Honoré de Balzac* (French novelist, 1790–1850)

    "Every calling is great when greatly pursued."
    —*Oliver Wendell Holmes, Jr.* (associate justice, U.S. Supreme Court, 1841–1935)

WRITING STRATEGY:
Quickwriting
See page 246.

    a. Quickwrite for five to ten minutes on the quotation of your choice.

    b. Look back over the readings in the unit for examples to illustrate your understanding of the quotation. Think also of examples from your own experience. List these in your journal.

    c. Tell a classmate about your response to the quotation. Listen to any ideas or questions that your classmate has.

WRITING STRATEGY:
Organizing Ideas
See page 245.

    d. Think of different ways you could organize your ideas in a piece of writing. Choose the way you like best.

    e. Write a first draft of your paper.

    f. Place a copy of your writing in your writing folder.

CHAPTER FOUR

Predicting Tomorrow's Jobs

1. **Class Work.** How would you answer the question below? List your ideas on the board. Then tell why you think people will be needed in these occupations.

WRITING STRATEGY:
Listing Ideas
See page 241.

Which Occupations Offer Tomorrow's Jobs?

Occupations	Why?
doctors	growing population
	more elderly people

2. **Class Work.** Scan the newspaper article on page 32–33 to find the occupations mentioned by the writer. Add these occupations to your chart in Activity 1. Then predict why people will be needed in these occupations.

READING STRATEGY:
Scanning
See page 254.

Reading for
Specific Information
See page 254.

3. **On your own.** As you read the article on pages 32–33, check your predictions from Activity 2. After you finish reading, add information from the article to your chart on the board.

Which Occupations Offer Tomorrow's Jobs?

by Mary Sit

from *The Boston Globe Career Guide*

Most career counselors tell their clients that the key to job satisfaction 1 is finding a line of work they are interested in and enjoy. But for those about to embark on a course of training or study that will take years to complete (usually at considerable expense), there is comfort in knowing there will be a demand for their skills down the road.

So we look to the U.S. Bureau of Labor Statistics for projections on the 2 occupations that will be most in demand over the next decade. Health care dominates as a hot career field with jobs expected to grow from 8.9 to 12.8 million between now and the year 2005. Outside the health-care field, here's what the Labor Department and futurists are picking:

EDUCATION. Teachers—primary and secondary and college levels—will be 3 needed. This may be surprising as cities and towns struggle with budget cuts and lay off[1] teachers. But the baby boomlet[2]—children of middle-aged baby boomers[3]—is hitting school age.

Between the years 1990 to 2005, elementary school age children will 4 increase by 3.8 million; secondary school age by 3.2 million; and post secondary school age by 1.4 million, according to the Bureau of Labor Statistics. In addition, foreign, older and part-time students will result in more post-secondary teaching positions. And there's a spillover[4] from the demand in education: teacher aides, counselors and administrative staff are expected to increase. All in all, the need for teachers is expected to add 2.3 million jobs in education by the year 2005.

---

1 **lay off**   terminate jobs
2 **baby boomlet**   period of high birth rate
3 **baby boomers**   people who were born during a period of high birth rate
4 **spillover**   secondary effect

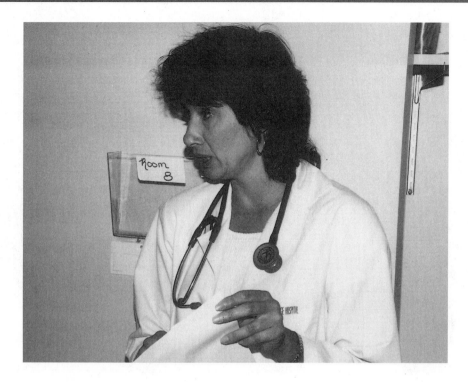

5 **FINANCIAL SERVICES.** Corporate jobs and entrepreneurship should do well in financial services—from accountants to market analysts, stock fund managers and stock brokers.

6   "We're moving from an industrially based economy to an information- ally based economy. And one of the most driving forces is finances," says Patricia Aberdeen, author of "Megatrends for Women."

7 **PARALEGAL SERVICES.** This is the second-fastest growing occupation, according to the Bureau of Labor Statistics. "We're a very litigious[5] society," says Mary Sullivan, regional economist at the U.S. Bureau of Labor Statistics. "There are many routine kinds of things lawyers are able to hire paralegals to do." People today are questioning whether they can get similar—but less expensive—services from paralegals.

8 **ENVIRONMENTAL PRESERVATION AND RENOVATION.** "We want to keep our environment pure and clean," says Edward Cornish, president of

---

5 **litigious**   ready to sue in court

World Future Society, a nonprofit group that studies sociological and technological trends.[6]

Any job that recycles, cleans up pollutants, preserves historic sites or restores forests will be a good pick, says Cornish. [9]

This extends as well to our internal environments, such as our homes. People are finally paying attention to issues beyond heating and cooling their homes and are concerned, for example, with radon[7] poisoning and lead paint. [10]

TRAVEL. This has become the world's leading industry, in terms of employing workers, says Cornish. Travel and the hospitality industry will offer more jobs as people become more affluent[8] and as technology makes transportation more comfortable and cheaper. [11]

EATING AND DRINKING ESTABLISHMENTS. This ranks as the third-fastest growing occupation under the services sector, says the U.S. Labor Department. Although many of these jobs are not career-oriented—waiters and dishwashers—others include jobs with money-making potential, such as managers and chefs, points out Sullivan. [12]

---

6 **trends**   directions
7 **radon**   a colorless, radioactive gas
8 **affluent**   rich

4. **Pair Work.** Choose the dictionary definition that best fits the meaning of the <u>underlined</u> words in the sentences below. Circle your answer. Then answer the questions that follow.

READING STRATEGY:
Using Context
See page 255.

a. "Most career counselors tell their clients that the <u>key</u> to job satisfaction is finding a line of work they are interested in and enjoy."

key *n* ❶ an instrument, usually made of metal, that one puts into a hole and turns, to lock or unlock a door, start or stop a car engine, etc. ❷ something that explains, answers, or helps you to understand: *Her unhappy childhood is the key to her character.* ❸ any of the parts in a writing or printing machine or musical instrument that are pressed down to make it work: *the keys of a piano* ❹ a set of musical notes based on a particular note: *a song in the key of C*

What do you think is the key to personal happiness?

_____

b. "But, for those people about to <u>embark</u> on a course of training or study that will take years to complete (usually at considerable expense), there is comfort in knowing there will be a demand for their skills down the road."

embark *v* ❶ to go, put, or take onto a ship: *We embarked at Montreal, and disembarked in New York a week later.* ❷ to start (something new): *to embark on a new way of life*

What advice would you give to someone who is embarking on a new career?

_____

c. "Health care <u>dominates</u> as a hot career field with jobs expected to grow from 8.9 to 12.8 million between now and the year 2005."

dominate *v* ❶ to have or exercise controlling power (over): *Her desire to dominate (other people) has caused trouble in her family.* ❷ to have the most important place or position (in): *Sports, and not learning, seem to dominate in that school.* ❸ to

35

rise or to be higher than; provide a view from a height above: *The church dominated the whole town.*

What language dominates in the field of international business?

_____

d. "Teachers—primary and secondary and college levels—will be needed. This may be surprising as cities and towns struggle with budget <u>cuts</u> and lay off teachers. But the baby boomlet—children of middle-aged baby boomers—is <u>hitting</u> school age."

cut *n* ❶ the result of cutting; an opening; wound: *a cut in the cloth/How did you get that cut on your hand?* ❷ something obtained by cutting: *cuts (=pieces) of fresh lamb* ❸ a reduction in size, amount, etc.: *cuts in government spending* ❹ *informal* a share: *The government plans to take a 50% cut of oil profits.*

hit *v* ❶ to give a blow to; strike: *He hit the other man.* ❷ to (cause to) come against something with force: *The ball hit the window.* ❸ *informal* to reach: *We hit the main road after traveling two miles on a side road.*

—*Definitions from* Longman Dictionary of American English

If you wanted to save some money, what cuts could you make in your current monthly budget?

_____

_____

_____

If the retirement age is 65, in what year will you hit retirement?

_____

Compare answers with your classmates.

36

5. **On your own.** Who does the writer quote in her article? Look back over the article to find these people. Then complete the chart below.

Source of quote	Credentials	Information (in your own words)
Patricia Aberdeen	author of "Megatrends for Women"	In the future, there will be jobs in financial services because we are moving towards an informationally based economy.

Share ideas about these people, as in the example below.

Example: *According to Patricia Aberdeen, author of "Megatrends for Women,"... .*

6. **On your own.** Imagine that you work for the U.S. Bureau of Labor Statistics and a young person writes to you for advice in choosing a career. Given your knowledge of the job market in the future, what advice would you give? Write your response in your journal.

CRITICAL THINKING
STRATEGY:
Analyzing
See page 258.

7. **Group Work.** Look at the article on pages 32–33 with a writer's eye. As you discuss each question below, take turns recording your group's ideas.

    a. Do you think the title of the article is effective? Why or why not?

    b. Where in the article does the writer identify the focus of her writing? Underline the sentence or sentences.

    c. How did the writer organize her ideas in this article?

    d. This article lacks a conclusion. What would you include in a conclusion to this article?

    Use your notes to report your group's ideas to the class.

8. **Writing Project.** In writing, tell your classmates about the occupations in demand in the area where you live now. Here are some suggestions to help you get started:

WRITING STRATEGY:
*Collecting
Information*
See page 238.

    a. Study the *Help Wanted* section of a local newspaper. (In some cities, the Sunday newspaper has the largest selection of jobs.) Look for the areas that offer today's jobs. That is, which areas (e.g., travel, health care) seem to need the most people? Within these areas, which occupations are advertised most frequently? Make a chart to record your observations.

WRITING STRATEGY:
Organizing Ideas
See page 245.

    c. Think of different ways to organize your ideas. Choose the way you like best.

    d. Write a first draft of your paper.

    e. Read Around. Get together with a group of classmates. Take turns reading each other's papers.

    f. Place a copy of your writing in your writing folder.

UNIT ONE
Final Project

You now have four pieces of writing in your writing folder, one from the writing assignment at the end of each chapter. Each piece of writing is a rough draft—a collection of first ideas.

Your final project is to revise one of these first drafts. You'll probably want to revise the one that interests you most. Before you start, though, read the notes below.

Notes on Revising

1. **What is revising?** *Revising* literally means *seeing again*. Think of revising as a process for developing your writing, not simply as a way to correct it.

2. **Who revises?** Every writer revises. As a writer, you must re-think and re-write in order to develop your ideas and explain them to a reader. Other people can help you edit your writing and polish it, but you are the only one who can actually revise your writing. Only you can adjust your writing to the vision forming in your head.

3. **Why does a writer revise?** Three basic aims are:
   • to sharpen your focus
   • to make your writing interesting to your readers
   • to help your readers follow your ideas

   Before you start revising your first draft from Unit One, think about how you can sharpen the focus of your writing. Here are some suggestions:

☑ *Revising to Sharpen Your Focus*

1. **Identify your audience.** Who are you writing for? Who will read your writing? Your classmates? Your teacher? Someone outside of class? Sometimes your audience is imaginary; your role might also be imaginary. For example, you might pretend to be a career counselor and your readers are teenagers who need advice on choosing careers.

2. **Limit your topic.** *Less is more* is the rule of thumb for writing in English. Don't try to tell everything you know. Instead, cover less ground and go deeply into your subject. Your audience will expect details. To make room for details, limit your topic.

Example:

Broad Topic	Limited Topic
careers	*qualities of a successful scientist*
	an ideal place to work
	occupations in demand today

3. **Cut out unnecessary words.** Most writers use too many words to make a point. That's not a problem in the first draft because it takes a lot of words to explore ideas. When you revise, though, economy becomes important. Pretend that you are sending a telegram and you must pay for every word. Read your draft to see which words don't advance your ideas and cut them out.

Example:

Before Revising

Some of the people in my classes and other people I know from school go to a place not so far from my school where they like to have coffee, meet their friends, and visit when they don't have classes.

After Revising

Some of my friends get together at a near-by coffeehouse between classes to drink coffee and socialize.

We asked Amanda Buege, an experienced writer, what she does to sharpen the focus of her writing. Here is what she said:

Revising to Sharpen Your Focus

A few days ago, I had some trouble. For some strange reason, I kept thinking about apple pie whenever I sat down to write. Ah, that flaky crust and scent of cinnamon! Why couldn't I get apple pie out of my head? I was supposed to be writing about how I revise to sharpen my focus.

Then I realized that it's a good idea to think about cooking and writing at the same time. After all, both take practice and time, and the results depend on the right blend[1] of ingredients. Cooking is a good metaphor[2] for writing. So what about that apple pie? Well, remember some key baking steps when you revise, and your essay will come out of the "oven" golden brown.

When I finish the first draft of my writing, I take a deep breath and relax. I've completed the hardest part. I always hope to have enough time before the next draft to let my writing "sit" for a day or two. My writing, like an apple, is ripening. Then I take out my paring knife.[3] The next step in writing, as well as in making an apple pie, is crucial. I must cut away the tough skin and remove any imperfections that would ruin a good essay. I try to be as objective as possible during this process. It helps to pretend that the writing actually belongs to someone else. "Is this sentence important? No? Then get rid of it." Sharpen your paring knife, and don't be afraid to cut.

Are you getting tired of my pie metaphor? I could extend it, but maybe I shouldn't. After all, I need to remember my audience. Then again, a good metaphor nearly always helps to clarify writing. Let's say I'm baking for Aunt Janice and Uncle Mark. Aunt Janice loves tart apples. Uncle Mark loves sweet apples with lots of nutmeg. Now is the time to sharpen my focus again, after I decide who will eat the most pie. Aunt Janice will probably have a big piece, but Uncle Mark will probably have seconds.[4] Now I have a better idea of what to put in my pie.

---

1 **blend**   combination
2 **metaphor**   using the characteristics of one thing to describe another, e.g., *He has the heart of a lion.*
3 **paring knife**   knife with a short blade, used for peeling fruit and vegetables
4 **seconds**   a second helping of food

☩║◇║☩║◇║☩║◇║☩║◇

ABOUT THE AUTHOR
Amanda Buege is a
graduate student and
teaching assistant in
the English
Department at the
University of New
Orleans. One of
Amanda's short stories
recently won first
place in a national
competition.

Try to examine your reading audience in the same way. Think about the tastes of your readers. If you want to win a blue ribbon[5] in a baking contest, make sure the judge (probably your teacher) likes the ingredients. Don't add any raisins—the dried up sentences that have no life and say very little. Use real butter instead of vegetable shortening. Lots of details make your writing rich.

Finally, limit the scope of your topic. You wouldn't try to cook a 15-course meal in two hours, would you? Don't try to discuss the world economy in detail when your city is voting on a tax increase. Keep your writing concise[6] and clear. Sometimes apple pie is best all by itself. Forget the ice cream. Bake and edit with a clear focus in mind. You'll produce the best results.

—*Amanda Buege*

5 **blue ribbon**   first-place in a competition
6 **concise**   expressing a lot in a few words

Process of Revising

Here are some suggestions to follow as you revise your first draft:

❖ Use the revising checklist on the next page to evaluate your first draft.

❖ From your evaluation, decide what changes you want to make. Note the changes in the margin of your paper. When you are ready, write a new draft.

❖ Ask a classmate to read your second draft and complete the revising checklist.

❖ Read through your draft several times. Make more notes in the margin of your draft, as you think of changes you want to make. When you are ready, write a new draft.

❖ Repeat any part of the process, making changes until you are satisfied with your writing. Your teacher may want to use the checklist to evaluate your final draft.

Unit One
Revising Checklist

Yes ✓

Sharpening your focus	First draft	Second draft	Third draft	Final draft
• Is it clear who the audience is?	❑	❑	❑	❑
• Is the topic limited enough?	❑	❑	❑	❑
• Have unnecessary words been deleted?	❑	❑	❑	❑

Your final draft might also be placed in a class booklet, along with your class-mates' writing. You can pass the booklet around for everyone to read.

UNIT TWO
Identity: Gender Roles

In this unit you will read four selections related to the theme of gender roles.

These photographs were taken in the United States more than 100 years ago.

- What do these pictures suggest about the roles of men and women in the past?
- How are these gender roles similar to or different from gender roles in your culture?
- In what ways are gender roles changing?

CHAPTER ONE

How Do We Learn Gender Roles?

1. **On your own.** In your culture, which of the workers below is more likely to be a man? Which is more likely to be a woman? Which is just as likely to be a man as a woman? Use a checkmark (✓) to indicate your answers.

	More likely to be a man	More likely to be a woman	As likely to be a man as a woman
Doctor	❏	❏	❏
Scientist	❏	❏	❏
Construction worker	❏	❏	❏
Teacher	❏	❏	❏
Child care worker	❏	❏	❏
Engineer	❏	❏	❏
University professor	❏	❏	❏
Chef in a restaurant	❏	❏	❏
Secretary	❏	❏	❏

What differences, if any, do you find in the jobs held by men and women? Tell your classmates. Together, think of reasons to explain these differences.

2. **Pair Work.** The sentences below are from the passage on pages 48–49. Read these sentences and look for a basic idea that connects them or is connected to all of them. Write your connecting idea on the lines below.

   a. "Look at the toys parents give to their children: Boys get tractors, trucks, tools, guns, and athletic equipment; girls get dolls, cooking sets, play perfume and cosmetic kits, and pretty clothes."

   b. "Textbooks portray boys in active, aggressive, so-called masculine roles and girls in passive, tender, so-called feminine roles."

   c. "A study of teachers in nursery schools found that they spent more time with the boys in the class than with the girls."

Connecting idea: _____

_____

Read your connecting idea to the class. Based on this information, what do you think the passage is about? Share ideas with your classmates.

3. **On your own.** As you read the passage on pages 48–49, underline the important ideas. In the margin, write down the key points in your own words.

READING STRATEGY:
Predicting
See page 253.

Finding Main Ideas
See page 250.

Learning Gender Roles

by Judson Landis

from *Sociology,* a textbook

Thirty pairs of parents were questioned within twenty-four hours after the birth of their first child. They were asked to "describe your baby as you would to a close relative." Hospital information on the babies showed that the fifteen boy babies and the fifteen girl babies did not differ *on such objective data as birth length, weight, irritability, etc. But the parents said that girl babies were softer, littler, more beautiful, prettier, more finely featured, cuter, and more inattentive than the boy babies. The fathers tended to label, or stereotype, the babies in this fashion more than the mothers. The authors of the study suggest that sex typing and sex-role socialization have already begun at birth.*

How could this be? One day and already babies are showing definite 1 gender differences in terms of physical appearance and temperament. The answer, of course, is that *it isn't so.* People assume that males and females are born with different abilities and temperaments. People assume it to be so, and then behave as if it *were* so. We tend to act toward children one way if they are male, another way if they are female. We expect them to be a certain way, and they turn out that way.

2   Like other roles, gender roles are learned through the socialization process. It is possible that in our society the teaching of gender roles starts even earlier than the teaching of other roles. As we saw above, parents immediately start acting differently toward their children based on their gender. Look at their toys: Boys get tractors, trucks, tools, guns, and athletic equipment; girls get dolls, cooking sets, play perfume and cosmetic kits, and pretty clothes.

3   The schools continue the pattern. Textbooks portray boys in active, aggressive, so-called masculine roles and girls in passive, tender, so-called feminine roles. A study of teachers in nursery schools[1] found that they spent more time with the boys in the class than with the girls. Boys were encouraged to work harder on academic subjects. They were given more rewards and more directions in how to do things. Boys were given instructions, then encouraged to complete the task themselves. If the girls did not quickly get the idea, the teacher would often intervene and do the task for them. There was one exception: The teachers did pay more attention to the girls on

Textbook, 1966. What is this textbook teaching about gender roles?

"Mark! Janet!" said Mother. "What is going on here?"

"She can not skate," said Mark. "I can help her. I want to help her. Look at her, Mother. Just look at her. She is just like a <u>girl</u>. She gives up,"

---

1 **nursery schools**   child-care centers

feminine gender-typed activities such as cooking. Even here girls got praise and assistance, whereas boys got detailed instructions. The boys were given more attention, and the environment was much more of a learning experience for them than it was for the girls. Studies have found the same thing: more attention to males than to females throughout the grades and a "let me do it for you" attitude toward females, even at the college level.

Another group of researchers working in the Boston area found that [4] gender-role differences were well developed in the majority of children by the age of five. The children knew which personality traits were "masculine" and which were "feminine." They knew which jobs were for men and which were for women. The experimenters developed a curriculum that attempted to make the children more flexible in their assumptions[2] about the sexes. The outcome of the program was mixed. To the researchers' surprise, many of the fifth- and ninth-grade boys with whom they worked became more stereotyped in their views of women and more rigid and outspoken about what they thought to be the woman's place. The effects on the girls in the program were more positive, showing attitude change away from typical stereotypes and increased self-esteem.[3]

The results of gender-role stereotyping are many and varied, and not all [5] the benefits are for males. The male is restricted in how he may show emotion: He is strong and silent, he does not show weakness, and he keeps his feelings under careful rein,[4] at least outwardly. The female has far greater freedom to express emotion. The male is subject to much more stress and pressure to achieve and be successful. This is probably part of the reason why males have a shorter life expectancy, more heart disease, and higher rates of suicide and hospitalization for mental illness. Women have been much less involved in crime and deviant[5] behavior than have men, and this too is related to gender-role differences. Some men would like to change roles and to be househusbands, staying home and cooking, working in the garden, and taking care of the kids. What are their chances in a society that sets up gender roles like ours does?

---

2 **assumptions**   beliefs
3 **self-esteem**   sense of one's own value
4 **under careful rein**   controlled, hidden
5 **deviant**   abnormal, not acceptable

4. **Pair Work.** Use context—the words and ideas around an unfamiliar word—to guess the meaning of the underlined words and phrases in the sentences below. Then look up each word in a dictionary and choose the definition that best fits the meaning of the word in this context.

READING STRATEGY:
Using Context
See page 255.

   a. "One day and already babies are showing definite gender differences in terms of physical appearance and temperament."

   My guess: _____

   Dictionary definition: _____

   b. "We tend to act toward children one way if they are male, another way if they are female. We expect them to be a certain way, and they turn out that way."

   My guess: _____

   Dictionary definition: _____

   c. "Like other roles, gender roles are learned through the socialization process. It is possible that in our society the teaching of gender roles starts even earlier than the teaching of other roles."

   My guess: _____

   Dictionary definition: _____

   d. "Boys were given instructions, then encouraged to complete the task themselves. If the girls did not quickly get the idea, the teacher would often intervene and do the task for them."

   My guess: _____

   Dictionary definition: _____

   e. "The outcome of the program was mixed. To the researchers' surprise, many of the fifth- and ninth-grade boys with whom they worked became more stereotyped in their views of women and more rigid and outspoken about what they thought to be the woman's place. The effects on the girls in the program were more positive, showing attitude change away from typical stereotypes and increased self-esteem."

My guess: _____

Dictionary definition: _____

Compare ideas with your classmates.

▚▚◈▐▚▚◈▐▚▚◈▐▚▚◈▐

READING STRATEGY:
*Taking Notes
in a Chart*
See page 255.

5. **Pair Work.** Use your margin notes and the information that you underlined (Activity 3) in the passage to complete the chart below. Try to use your own words.

Paragraph	Topic	Summary of Information
1	gender differences	Gender differences are learned.
2	learning gender roles	Parents start teaching their children gender roles from a very early age.
3	learning gender roles	
4		
5		

Compare charts with your classmates.

52

6. **On your own.** Use your chart from Activity 5 to write a summary of the article. Consider the following information as you write your summary:

   • Your summary should be no more than one-fourth the length of the original article.

   • Use your own words to present the author's main ideas and key points.

   • Don't include unnecessary details in your summary.

   • Begin your summary with a reference to the author and source of the article.

   Exchange summaries with a classmate. Check to see if you included the same important points from the article.

> **READING STRATEGY:**
> *Summarizing*
> See page 254.

7. **Pair Work.** Find examples in the passage to support the statement below.

   Gender roles are learned through the socialization process.

   ### Example:

   Parents give different toys to male children and female children.

   _____

   _____

   _____

   _____

   _____

   _____

   _____

   _____

   Compare answers with another pair.

> **WRITING STRATEGY:**
> *Giving Examples*
> See page 240.

READING STRATEGY:
Reading for Specific Information
See page 254.

8. **Pair Work.** According to Judson Landis (pages 48–49), what qualities and characteristics are traditionally assigned to males and to females? Read through the passage and list your findings below. Then compare ideas with another pair.

What qualities and characteristics are traditionally assigned to males and to females?

Males	Females
active	*passive*

CRITICAL THINKING STRATEGY:
Comparing
See page 260.

9. **On your own.** The article on pages 48–49 deals with the teaching of gender roles in the United States. Compare and contrast this socialization process with the teaching of gender roles in your culture. List the similarities and differences.

Example:

In my culture, parents give different toys to male and female children just as parents in the United States do.

_____

_____

_____

_____

_____

_____

Read your sentences to a partner.

10. **On your own.** Choose an idea in the passage that interests you. Connect this idea to your own experience and write your ideas in your journal. Here are some questions you can think about as you write:

    • What does this idea remind you of from your own experience?

    • Based on your experience, do you agree or disagree with this idea? Why?

CRITICAL THINKING
STRATEGY:
Synthesizing
See page 263.

11. **Group Work.** Look at the article with a writer's eye. As you discuss the questions below, take turns recording your group's ideas.

    a. How does this writer focus his ideas on the topic of gender roles?

    b. Why do you think the writer included the italicized information at the beginning of the article?

    c. How many main ideas does the writer develop? How do you know which ideas are "main" ideas?

    d. How does the writer develop the main ideas?

    Use your notes to report your group's ideas to the class.

CRITICAL THINKING
STRATEGY:
Analyzing
See page 258.

12. **Writing Project.** How do people learn gender roles? Write your answer to this question for someone outside of class to read— someone who has not read the passage by Judson Landis. Use ideas from the article by Landis, from other material you have read, and from your own experience. Here are some suggestions you can follow to get started:

    a. Focus on the question *How do people learn gender roles?* and note any answers from the article on pages 48–49. Be sure to cite your source.

    Example: *According to Judson Landis, parents act differently towards their children based on their gender.*

WRITING STRATEGY:
Citing Sources
See page 237.

⬛❚◈❚⬛❚◈❚⬛❚◈⬛❚◈

WRITING STRATEGY:
Quickwriting
See page 246.

b. Consider how you learned about gender roles. Quickwrite in your journal for ten minutes. Use the questions below to help you get started.

- What toys did you play with as a child? Did children of the opposite gender play with the same toys?

- In school, did teachers treat girls and boys differently? If so, how?

- Was there anything that you weren't allowed to do because of your gender?

c. Tell a partner how you learned about gender roles. Answer any questions your partner has.

⬛❚◈❚⬛❚◈❚⬛❚◈⬛❚◈

WRITING STRATEGY:
Focusing Your Ideas
See page 239.

Organizing Ideas
See page 245.

d. List the ideas that you might want to include in your writing. From your list, choose one or two main ideas to focus on. Then think of other examples and details to help you develop your main ideas.

e. Think of different ways you might organize these ideas in a piece of writing.

f. Write a first draft of your paper.

g. Ask a friend outside of class to read your paper. Answer any questions your friend has about the information in your paper. Take notes on ideas that come up.

h. Place a copy of your writing and your notes in your writing folder.

CHAPTER TWO

Do Men and Women "Speak" the Same Body Language?

1. Class Work. People use body language—facial expressions, gestures, and body movements—to communicate. Based on the body language of the people in these pictures, what information do you think they are communicating?

CRITICAL THINKING
STRATEGY:
Analyzing
See page 258.

2. **Group Work.** In the photograph below, one person is the employer (the boss) and one is the employee. Which do you think is which? How does their body language help you to guess? Share your group's ideas with the class.

3. **Group Work.** *Affiliative cues* are facial expressions and body movements that indicate a subordinate (lower or less important) position. *Power cues,* on the other hand, indicate a more important or powerful position. Which of these examples of body language do you think is an affiliative cue? Which is a power cue? Classify your ideas on the tree diagram below.

CRITICAL THINKING STRATEGY: *Classifying* See page 260.

Examples:

WRITING STRATEGY: *Making a Tree Diagram* See page 244.

smiling	serious facial expressions	nodding your head
frowning	direct eye contact	extending your legs
	tilting your head	lowering your eyes

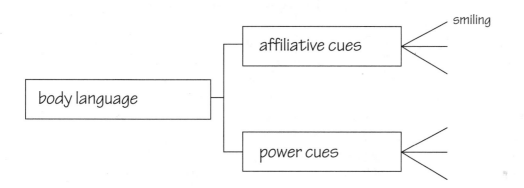

Share your group's ideas with the class.

4. **Class Work.** Read the title of the article on page 60 and look the pictures over. Based on this information, how do you think this article might relate to the theme of gender roles? What do you think the article is about?

5. **On your own.** As you read the article, underline the important ideas. You might also want to write your thoughts and questions in the margin.

READING STRATEGY: *Predicting* See page 253.

Writing Margin Notes See page 257.

Body Language Speaks Louder Than Words

by Janet Lee Mills

from *Horizons*

I am a professional body watcher, and I love to turn others into body 1
watchers, too. And that is precisely what I do in my university classes and in
executive training seminars.

As a specialist in male-female communications, I propose that males and 2
females in our culture speak different body languages. To illustrate this point
I recruited Richard Friedman, Assistant to the President at the University of
Cincinnati, to model with me for the accompanying photographs. The photos
in which Friedman and I posed[1] in our usual male and female roles, respec-
tively, were easy. Then came the hard part, the part that proves my point. I
posed us in postures[2] typical of the opposite sex. The results in the photos illustrate the old maxim, "One picture is worth a thousand words."

The photos contain two basic sets of behavioral cues—affiliative cues 3
and power cues. Male nonverbal behavior typically includes very few affiliative displays, such as smiles and head cants,[3] and many power cues, such as
expanded limb positions and serious facial expressions. Female nonverbal
behavior, however, is ordinarily just the opposite, containing many affiliative displays and few power cues. The overall impression males create is one
of power, dominance, high status, and activity, particularly in contrast to the
overall impression females create, which is one of submission,[4] subordina-
tion, low status, and passivity.[5]

Sensitizing students and professional groups to these sex-role differ- 4
ences and the functions they serve in social and business contexts is my
business. In my seminars, I illustrate how men spread out their upper and
lower limbs, expanding to take up space; how men sit and stand in loose,
relaxed postures; how they gesture widely, speak in loud, deep tones, and

---

1 **posed**   stand or sit in a particular way for a photograph
2 **postures**   ways of holding the body
3 **head cants**   titled heads
4 **submission**   obedience; accepting someone else's power
5 **passivity**   inactivity

left: Ah, but doesn't Mills look feminine in this typically feminine pose with tilted head, affiliative smile, ankles crossed, hands folded.

right: And doesn't Friedman look ridiculous in the same pose?

left: The author demonstrates a typical male pose. Women in business clothes appear shocking in this pose.

right: Friedman does not appear shocking in the same pose, since many business executives conduct business from a similar position.

engage in either direct or detached eye-contact patterns. All these behaviors communicate power and high status, especially when men are communicating with subordinates. I also illustrate how women constrict their arms and legs; sit in attentive, upright postures; gesture diminutively;[6] speak in soft, breathy voices; and lower their eyes frequently. These behaviors give away power and announce low status.

---

6 **diminutively**   with small movements

Mills is famous for this photo, which she captions, "Could you say no to this woman?" In it she poses in a posture typical of the opposite sex.

In addition, I point out to audiences that women smile often, cant their heads, nod their heads, open their eyes in wide-eyed wonder, and posture themselves in positions of unstable balance. Men return smiles or not, at will,[7] engage in far less head canting and nodding, keep their eyes relaxed, and posture themselves in stable balance. 3

These sex differences are socially learned and publicly performed, but are relatively unconscious in both the sender and receiver—until someone breaks the rules or norms. But when the rules are broken all attention is focused on the person breaking them. 4

Women in management are of particular concern to me. Managerial and professional women simultaneously play two roles, that of "woman" and that of "manager" (or professor, doctor, accountant, and so forth). And the role of woman and the role of manager or professional each has a different set of rules—contradictory[8] rules. From the depths of sex-role socialization comes the demand "be feminine," but from the context of the managerial work place comes the demand "be powerful." 5

But there is a way for women to extricate[9] themselves and rise to the top of the corporate ladder[10] with their femininity intact. To succeed ultimately requires the simultaneous expression of both femininity and power. This involves a collapsing of the two inconsistent roles into a unified whole. The nonverbal behaviors of the women in this state include both messages of affiliation and power, delivered simultaneously. She smiles as she looks you straight in the eye. She spreads out her arms, cants her head, knits her brows in thought, and speaks with clear diction. 6

And now a challenge: If you are a woman, assume the masculine poses pictured here; if you are a man, assume the female poses on these pages. By actually experiencing poses typical of those of the opposite sex, you may gain new insight[11] into your own sex-role training—and learn to know a thing by its opposite. 7

---

7 **at will**   as they wish
8 **contradictory**   opposing
9 **extricate**   get out of a difficult situation
10 **corporate ladder**   hierarchy of jobs and power
11 **insight**   understanding

6. **On your own.** Choose three words in the article that are new to you. Use one or more of these strategies to learn the meaning of each word:

   a. Try using context to guess the meaning of the word.

   b. Ask a friend what the word means.

   c. Look up the word in a dictionary.

   Write your own sentences, using the words that you chose. Provide context clues to help your readers understand the meaning of each word. Then read your sentences aloud and ask your classmates to guess the meaning of the words.

   Example: *If we talk <u>simultaneously</u>, we won't be able to understand each other.*

READING STRATEGY:
Using Context
See page 255.

7. **Group Work.** Share ideas about the article. Choose three of the questions below to discuss in your group.

   a. What examples of affiliative and power cues does the writer, Janet Mills, give? List them in the chart below.

CRITICAL THINKING
STRATEGY:
Analyzing
See page 258.

Affiliative cues	Power cues
canted head	

   b. Look again at your tree diagram in Activity 3. How accurate were your guesses?

   c. Look again at the picture in Activity 2. Based on the information in the reading, which person is probably the boss? Why do you think so?

d. Roleplay a conversation in which these people participate:

- someone who uses mainly power cues

- someone who uses mainly affiliative cues

- someone who simultaneously uses power and affiliative cues

e. Try the challenge described at the end of the reading. Then tell how you felt taking the pose of the opposite gender.

8. **On your own.** If you were going to take a job in management in the United States, would you change the way you use body language? Why or why not? Explore these questions as you write in your journal.

⬛⬛⬛⬛⬛⬛⬛⬛⬛⬛⬛

READING STRATEGY:
*Taking Notes
in a Chart*
See page 255.

9. **On your own.** Use your margin notes and the ideas that you underlined in the article to complete the chart below. Be sure to use your own words.

Paragraph	Topic	Summary of Information
1	author's occupation	The author teaches people about body language in her university classes and in training seminars.
2		
3		
4		
5		
6		
7		
8		
9		

Compare charts with your classmates.

10. **On your own.** Write a summary of the article "Body Language Speaks Louder Than Words." Keep these ideas in mind as you write your summary:

> **READING STRATEGY:**
> *Summarizing*
> See page 254.

- Your summary should be no more than one-fourth the length of the original article.

- Use your own words to present main ideas and key points.

- Don't include unnecessary details in your summary.

- Begin your summary with a reference to the author and source of the article.

Example:

According to Janet Lee Mills, the author of "Body Language Speaks Louder Than Words,"… .

11. **Group Work.** Look at the reading with a writer's eye. As you discuss the questions below, take turns recording your group's ideas.

> **CRITICAL THINKING STRATEGY:**
> *Analyzing*
> See page 258.

   a. Do you think the introduction is effective? Why or why not?

   b. What is the thesis, or most comprehensive idea? Is the thesis stated directly? If so, where?

   c. How does the writer support her argument? Do you think she provides enough support?

   d. How does the writer conclude her article? Do you think it is an effective conclusion? Why or why not?

Use your notes to report your group's ideas to the class.

12. **Writing Project.** A foreign company wants to do business in the United States. This company has hired you to write a two-page paper for its employees to read. The purpose of your paper is to help the male and female employees use effective body language when dealing with American businesspeople. Here are some suggestions you can follow to help you get started:

▓▒▪║◇║▪▒◇║▪▒║◇║▪▒║◇

WRITING STRATEGY:
*Understanding
Your Audience*
See page 247.

a. Think about your audience. What country/culture are they from? Write down some questions you think they will want you to answer.

b. What are the most important things that your audience needs to know about using body language when dealing with American businesspeople? List the important points you want to make in your two-page paper.

c. Look back through your notes from the activities in this chapter. Write down any words, phrases, or ideas that you might want to use in your writing. Be sure to keep track of your sources.

d. For five to ten minutes, quickwrite about the topic of your paper.

e. Using your notes and your quickwriting, write a first draft of your paper.

f. Place a copy of your writing in your writing folder.

CHAPTER THREE

What Happens When Gender Roles Conflict Across Cultures?

1. **On your own.** Imagine that you are married to someone from a different culture. How might your understanding of the role of a husband or wife differ from that of your spouse? What problems might this cause? Explore these questions as you write in your journal.

2. **Class Work.** Read the title and the first paragraph of the newspaper article on page 68 and then answer the questions below.

   a. What does the title of the article mean to you?

   b. What do you think the writer means when he says "America is coming between me and my 12-year-old son"?

   c. How might this article be connected to the theme of gender roles?

READING STRATEGY: *Previewing* See page 253.

3. **On your own.** As you read the article, underline the ideas you think are important. You might also want to write your thoughts and questions in the margin.

READING STRATEGY: *Writing Margin Notes* See page 257.

The Americanization of George

by Samir Khalaf

from *The Christian Science Monitor*

America is coming between me and my 12-year-old son. Actually, it started earlier, when George was hardly 10. Since then, I have helplessly watched this incursion,[1] often with dismay and alarm.

Over two years ago we escaped the horrors of Lebanon, and chose quiet Princeton over the vibrancy[2] of Harvard.... But little did I know that he was to face, at such an early age, the more subtle "terror" of American peer pressure[3] and the unsettling dissonance[4] of conflicting norms and expectations.

The family system in Lebanon is, on the whole, intimate, warm, and affectionate. A child there grows up in a nurturing[5] atmosphere of extended kinship networks.

The Lebanese, much like adjacent Mediterranean cultures, are very tactile. Touching, kissing, hugging, and the outward display of emotion—regardless of gender—are generously and spontaneously expressed. At least children of George's age indulge in these emotive expressions[6] with little self-consciousness or feelings of shame or guilt.

I first noticed a change in George upon returning from a brief trip a few months after we had settled in Princeton. Normally, even after the regular daily return home from work, George would interrupt his play and rush across the driveway to greet me; often, he would literally hurl himself into my open arms.

---

1 **incursion** invasion, unwelcome entry
2 **vibrancy** high energy
3 **peer pressure** influence of people your age
4 **dissonance** discord, lack of harmony
5 **nurturing** with loving care
6 **emotive expressions** communication of feelings

6   On that day, however, just as he was about to follow his normal impulse as he rushed across the driveway, he suddenly "froze" in mid-passage and looked in the direction of his watchful playmates. With obvious hesitation and embarrassment, he calmly walked over to greet me with a cold handshake and a casual "Hi, Dad." Bit by bit, even this gesture has been abandoned.

7   Such frozen moments have recurred and spilled over to other daily encounters with members of the family, and in particular acquaintances from Lebanon. I could see him fret as relatives and friends he has not seen for two years try, in vain,[7] to solicit a hug or a kiss on the forehead. The reluctant denial has been transformed into a boast, that he is now an "American boy."

8   His "Americanization" was most forcefully conveyed by a recent incident on the tennis court. We were struggling in a doubles game against two other, more experienced partners who normally beat us. After a long and heated game we won the set, partly because of two exquisite shots by George. He was ecstatic. As he rushed across to share his exuberance with me Lebanese style, he "froze" once again and treated me to a tamed version of the American "high five."[8]

---

7 **in vain**   without success
8 **high five**   hitting your open hand against someone else's to express solidarity

READING STRATEGY:
Using Context
See page 255.

4. On your own. Find the italicized words below in the article on pages 68–69. Use context to guess the meaning of each word. Then think about the answer to the question that follows. After you finish, compare ideas with a classmate.

a. Paragraph #1: *helplessly*

My guess: _____

Why do you think the writer of the article feels <u>helpless</u>?

b. Paragraph #4: *tactile*

My guess: _____

What is an example of a <u>tactile</u> display of emotion?

c. Paragraph #5: *hurl*

My guess: _____

Why do you think George <u>hurled</u> himself into his father's arms?

d. Paragraph #7: *fret*

My guess: _____

How might George have shown that he was <u>fretting</u>?

e. Paragraph #8: *beat*

My guess: _____

How do you feel when someone <u>beats</u> you at a game?

CRITICAL THINKING STRATEGY:
Interpreting
See page 262.

5. Group Work. Share ideas about the article. As you answer the questions below, take notes on your group's discussion.

a. In what way is George being Americanized? How does his father feel about this?

b. From whom is George learning about gender roles in the United States?

c. What do you think will happen to George as he grows older? How might he deal with the cultural differences?

Get together with another group and share your answers.

6. **On your own.** Think again about the writer's statement that "America is coming between me and my 12-year-old son." What does this statement mean to you now? For five to ten minutes, quickwrite in your journal.

WRITING STRATEGY:
Quickwriting
See page 246.

7. **Pair Work.** Reread the fifth and sixth paragraphs in the article. What inferences can you make about George and his friends? Write your ideas on the lines below.

READING STRATEGY:
Making Inferences
See page 252.

a. What inferences can you make about George?

_____

_____

_____

b. What inferences can you make about his playmates?

_____

_____

_____

Get together with your classmates and compare ideas.

8. **Group Work.** Look at the article with a writer's eye. As you discuss the questions below, take turns recording your group's ideas.

CRITICAL THINKING STRATEGY:
Analyzing
See page 258.

a. Do you think the introduction to this article is effective? Why or why not?

b. What is the main point?

c. Does the writer provide details to illustrate his main point? Give an example.

d. Do you have any questions that you wish the writer had answered?

9. **Writing Project.** How would you describe gender roles in your culture? What personality traits are considered to be "masculine"? What personality traits are considered to be "feminine"? What types of behavior might be considered unusual or inappropriate for a man or a woman? Explore these questions as you prepare to write a two-page paper telling your classmates about gender roles in your culture. Here are some other suggestions to help you get started:

a. Spend time collecting information about gender roles in your culture. Try one or more of these activities:

- Get together with a partner. Answer your partner's questions about gender roles in your culture. Take notes on the ideas that come up during the discussion.

- Quickwrite in response to the questions above. Then go back over your writing and circle any ideas that you might want to include in your paper.

- Get together with someone from your culture and share ideas about gender roles.

b. Think about how you might focus the topic of your paper. Instead of telling everything you know about gender roles, choose one or two important points to write about.

c. Think of details and examples you can use to illustrate the points you want to cover in your paper. List these in your journal.

d. Think of different ways you might organize your writing. Choose the way you like best.

e. Write a first draft of your paper.

f. Exchange papers with a partner. Listen to any questions your partner has and take notes.

g. Place a copy of your paper, with your notes, in your writing folder.

WRITING STRATEGY:
Collecting Information
See page 238.

WRITING STRATEGY:
Focusing Your Ideas
See page 239.

Giving Examples
See page 240.

CHAPTER FOUR

What Are the Effects of Gender Stereotyping?

1. **Class Work.** Read these definitions of the word *stereotype*. Then think of several examples of gender stereotyping and write them on the lines below.

WRITING STRATEGY:
Listing Ideas
See page 241.

stereotype *n* a fixed pattern which represents a type of person or event: *He's the stereotype of an army officer.*

stereotype *v* **-typed, -typing** to think of (a thing or person) as a representative of a particular type and not as an individual: *She has a stereotyped view of teachers, believing that they are all as bad as hers were.*

Examples of gender stereotyping

Women are emotional
_____

Men aren't good listeners.
_____

_____

_____

_____

_____

_____

_____

2. **Class Work.** Read the first three paragraphs of the short story on page 75. What examples of gender stereotyping do you find in these paragraphs? Share ideas with your classmates.

READING STRATEGY:
Previewing
See page 253.

3. **Pair Work.** Based on the information in the first three paragraphs, how would you answer the question in the title? On the lines below, list what you know about Emma Hu. Then compare ideas with your classmates.

Who's Hu?

_____

_____

_____

_____

_____

_____

READING STRATEGY:
Writing Margin Notes
See page 257.

4. **On your own.** As you read the story, underline the parts of the story that bring up issues of gender roles. In the margin, write any thoughts or questions that come to mind as you read.

Who's Hu?

by Lensey Namioka

1   I was tired of being a freak.[1]

2   My father was a professor of mathematics at M.I.T., and whenever I got 100 on my math test (which was pretty often) my high school teachers would say, "I know where Emma Hu gets help with her homework…cackle[2]…cackle… ." The rest of the class usually cackled along. At first I didn't see why they were so nasty about it. Later I discovered that girls in this country weren't supposed to be good in math. The teachers didn't like it when Arthur Aldrich—our self-styled math genius—corrected their mistakes in class. They hated it a lot more when I did.

3   In China there was nothing wrong with girls being good at math. In fact, Chinese women were supposed to keep the household or business accounts. But in America, when I opened my big mouth to correct my algebra teacher—in broken English, yet—everyone thought I was a freak. Once I thought I would cheat on my math test by deliberately making a couple of mistakes, but when it came to the point, I just couldn't do it. Mathematics was too beautiful to mess up.

4   On most days I wasn't too bothered by my math grades, but lately I had begun to worry. I was a senior at Evesham High, a high school in the suburbs of Boston, and the senior prom was only three weeks away. Who was going to ask a Chinese girl math whiz?[3] According to my friend Katey, everybody went to the prom except freaks.

5   After lunch the first class I attended was math. Just being in the classroom made me feel better. I liked to look around the room at the portion of the blackboard painted with a permanent white grid for graphing equations, the hanging cardboard models of regular polyhedra we had made as a class project, and the oak shelf containing plaster models of conic sections and various surfaces. My favorite was the hyperbolic paraboloid, or saddle, with its straight lines neatly incised in the plaster.

6   The class was Advanced Mathematics, intended for seniors who were going into science or math and who had already taken algebra, geometry,

---

1 **freak**   a strange or weird person
2 **cackle**   shrill laughter
3 **whiz**   genius

and trig. The course covered analytic geometry, calculus, and a little probability theory. Actually, it wasn't so much the content of the course that I liked best: it was the teacher, Mr. Antonelli. He was a short man only a little taller than I, and he had a swarthy face dominated by a huge beak of a nose. Unlike my other math teachers (one of them even a woman), he didn't seem to find it bizarre that a girl should do well in his class. As for my being Chinese, I doubt if he even noticed. Mr. Antonelli didn't care if you were a Martian eunuch,[4] as long as you did the math correctly.

Today Mr. Antonelli gave the impression of suppressed excitement. 7 He clearly had something on his mind, because for the first time I remember, he let one of the boys do a maximum-minimum problem without checking the second derivative to see if it was an inflection point. Arthur Aldrich and I beat each other to a draw[5] in pointing out the mistake. Mr. Antonelli acknowledged our reproof almost absentmindedly. He certainly was preoccupied.

With five minutes left of the period, Mr. Antonelli made an announce- 8 ment: "Class, you remember that last fall you all took the semi-final exam for the Sterns Mathematics Prize. Today I received word of the results."

The Sterns was a mathematics prize given annually to a high school 9 senior in Massachusetts. The award was for $200, but the prestige it carried was immeasurable. Never in the history of the Sterns Prize had it been won by a girl.

"Now," Mr. Antonelli went on, "it is an honor for our school if a student 10 here makes it to the finals. Well, we've got not just one student, but two who are going into the finals. One is Arthur Aldrich."

Arthur was a tall, gangly[6] boy with hair so blond that it looked almost 11 white. With his long nose and sharp chin, he reminded me of a white fox in one of the Chinese fairy tales. Arthur had very few stumbling blocks[7] in his life. His family was comfortably off,[8] he did well in every subject in school, and he was a credit to the Evasham High School track team. In spite of his successes, Arthur was too arrogant[9] to be popular.

"The other," Mr. Antonelli announced, "is Emma Hu." 12

The class cheered. My thoughts were in a whirl. I thought I had fallen 13 down badly on the exam the previous fall because there were two problems I hadn't been able to do. Now it seemed that my performance hadn't been so bad after all.

---

4 **eunuch** a man who has had part of his sex organs removed
5 **beat each other to a draw** tied, were even
6 **gangly** tall, thin, and ungraceful
7 **stumbling blocks** barriers
8 **comfortably off** without financial problems
9 **arrogant** too proud

14   I have only the vaguest memories of my other classes that afternoon. I barely realized when the final bell rang. Leaving school, I almost hugged my books to my chest. It was like waking up on my birthday and finding a pile of presents outside my door.

15   My mother probably felt like this when she looked over a new piece of music, and my father when he received a new set of Chinese pulp novels.

16   I was so absorbed that I didn't hear footsteps coming up behind me. I jumped when Arthur's voice spoke in my ear. "I want to talk to you."

17   "About what?" I asked, surprised. To my knowledge he had never asked any girl to anything before. In Arthur's ranking of animal intelligence, girls came somewhere between sheep and myna birds. Of course that made me even more of a freak in his eyes.

18   When he had seen that I threatened to become a rival,[10] Arthur began a systematic campaign to discourage me. In this he had the support of our previous math teachers. They kept hinting that for a girl to do well in math was unfeminine, unnatural, and unattractive.

19   At first I hadn't been too bothered. My English had been shaky,[11] and subtle hints were lost on me. Anyway, being teased about my math had been submerged in the larger misery of being an alien.[12] But by my junior year at Evasham, I began to be really uncomfortable. In my trig class I made a lot of mistakes in looking up trigonometric functions, and my math grade slid.[13] My parents were disturbed but couldn't think of a reason. It was my older brother, Emerson, who had looked over my homework papers and found my mistakes. He insisted on having my eyes checked, and when I turned out to have 20-20 vision,[14] he gave me a stern lecture and told me to shape up. My grades went back up.

20   In our Advanced Mathematics class, Arthur had found no support from the teacher, Mr. Antonelli. Although Mr. Antonelli was a wonderful teacher, his manner was dry and impersonal. He kept personalities out of the classroom entirely.

21   By using our last names, he made me forget I was the only girl in a class with eight boys. He also made all of us feel very adult.

22   Arthur grinned now. In the illustrations of my Chinese fairy tale book, foxes grinned with their mouths forming a big V. Arthur's smile was just like that. "I hear you want to go to the senior prom but can't find anyone to take you. I have a simple proposition to make: I'll take you to the

---

10 **rival**   opponent
11 **shaky**   not strong; not good
12 **alien**   foreigner
13 **slid**   went down
14 **20-20 vision**   perfect eyesight

prom—refreshments, corsage, dinner afterward, the whole works—if you'll drop out of[15] the Sterns exam."

The sheer gall[16] of his proposition took my breath away, and for a moment I was too astounded even to be angry. In the end my main reaction turned out to be triumph. "So you're really afraid I might do better than you on the exam!" I said, unable to hide my satisfaction. 23

Two spots of color appeared on Arthur's pale cheeks, but he kept his foxy grin. "I can do better than you any day, don't you worry! But I know you're desperate to go to the prom. Every red-blooded, normal high school senior goes to the prom, right?" 24

I said nothing. The price of being a red-blooded, normal high school senior was pretty high. 25

"Well?" demanded Arthur. 26

I was determined to be equally curt. "No," I said. 27

He stormed away[17] without another word. 28

"I'm terribly sorry. I couldn't help overhearing." 29

I turned around and saw it was Kim. He was a Korean boy who was one of my mother's music students. 30

It was almost a relief not to have to pretend. "It doesn't matter," I said. To my fury, my lips were beginning to quiver.[18] "There isn't a person in school who doesn't already know I haven't been able to find a date for the prom. It's been a joke for so long that I don't even feel humiliated about it anymore." 31

But that was a lie. 32

Kim looked as if he were trying not to laugh. "I don't even try to understand all these American customs anymore. But this prom sounds like some sort of native ritual or tribal dance." 33

He was a foreigner in America and not bothered by it at all. He was even inviting me to join him in enjoying the amusing antics[19] of the natives. 34

"Don't you feel lonely sometimes?" I asked, remembering my loneliness the first day of school on discovering I was to be the only Chinese there. That loneliness I suffered until Katey and her friends took me in.

Kim only smiled and shook his head. "I'm too busy. Schoolwork is hard for me because of my poor English, and after school all my time is taken up with practicing. Even if I had the money, I wouldn't go." He looked at me curiously. "You are devoted to mathematics the way I am to music, aren't you? I think I heard your mother say so." 35

---

15 **drop out of**   leave; decide not to participate in
16 **gall**   rude boldness; impudence
17 **stormed away**   left angrily
18 **quiver**   tremble; shake
19 **antics**   strange behavior

36   I nodded, grateful for these words. He considered our situations to be comparable, and he didn't think that a girl being interested in math was any stranger than a boy being interested in music.

37   As Kim got on his bus, he said, "You should try to do the best you can on the exam. You owe it to yourself."

❖

38   On the appointed afternoon, I entered the Boston University classroom where the Sterns examination was being held. The monitor checked my name against his list and nodded. "Good. All fifty of you are now here."

39   It seemed I was the last one to arrive. For a while I had considered not coming at all. What was the point? I was in no condition to do mathematics. I suppose I came because it would have been too much trouble to tell Mr. Antonelli I was planning to drop out.

40   We all sat down and arranged our pencils and bluebooks on the desks in front of us. When the monitor passed out the exams, heads bent eagerly over the papers. I looked at the first page with dull despair. There were some diagrams with circles, but nothing made sense to me. In my present state I hardly knew the difference between an ellipse and a circle. An ellipse was just a tired circle.

41   All around me pencils scratched busily in bluebooks. My pencil was still as I relived my private hell at home. On my left, Arthur glanced up at me. He looked different, and I realized he had applied a pomade on his hair to stick it down. He flashed his foxy grin, and the smugness in it told me I looked a mess. I had not slept at all the night before, and my eyes were red and puffy—not all from sleeplessness.

42   My watch showed that almost an hour had passed. Already half the time allotted for the exam was gone and I hadn't started a single problem.

43   I glanced at Arthur again and found his eyes fastened on me eagerly. How many times had he looked this way? He must have noticed that I hadn't done a thing, because when his eyes met mine, his grin widened triumphantly.

44   I picked up the exam paper and looked at it once more. The writing might as well have been in Greek. Only I could read Greek a little, since I already knew all the Greek letters from seeing them used in mathematics. No, the writing here might as well be in Korean for all I could understand.

45   Kim entered my mind. He could not afford to give up classical music, for he owed it to himself not to squander[20] his talent.

46   It was the thought of Kim that finally opened my eyes. I should not

---

20 **squander** waste

try to be something I was not. And I was not, nor could ever be, a normal American teenager. I was going to be a mathematician. This was the Sterns exam, my first opportunity to show my mettle.[21] I could not afford to squander my talent. As Kim had said, I owed it to myself. I had to stop frittering[22] away the precious minutes and get down to work. Having made the decision, I felt a weight lift from my chest.

---

21 **mettle**   courage
22 **frittering**   wasting

ABOUT THE AUTHOR

Lensey Namioka is a Chinese American writer who is known for her historical and fantasy stories. The story "Who's Hu?" is an excerpt from a novel of the same name.

5. **On your own.** Choose an idea, event, character, or line in the story that interests you. For several minutes, explore your thoughts about it. Here are some questions you can think about as you write.

   • Why is this interesting to you?

   • What questions does this part of the story raise for you?

   • Does this make you think of something or someone from your own experience? If so, what or whom?

6. **Pair Work.** Collect ideas and information from the story. Make an outline like this:

   READING STRATEGY:
   Making a Story Outline
   See page 251.

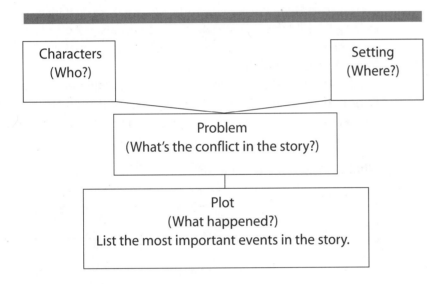

   Characters (Who?)

   Setting (Where?)

   Problem (What's the conflict in the story?)

   Plot (What happened?) List the most important events in the story.

   Compare outlines with another pair. Then use your outline to summarize the story orally. Take turns giving information.

7. **Pair Work.** What inferences can you make about the characters in the story based on the lines below?

   a. "Unlike my other math teachers…, he [Mr. Antonelli] didn't seem to find it bizarre that a girl should do well in his class. As for my being Chinese, I doubt if he even noticed."

   What can you infer about Mr. Antonelli?

   READING STRATEGY:
   Making Inferences
   See page 252.

b. "I have only the vaguest memories of my other classes that afternoon. I barely realized when the final bell rang. Leaving school, I almost hugged my books to my chest. It was like waking up on my birthday and finding a pile of presents outside my door."

What can you infer about the narrator? How does she feel?

_____

c. "'Don't you feel lonely sometimes?' I asked,...
Kim only smiled and shook his head. 'I'm too busy. Schoolwork is hard for me because of my poor English, and after school all my time is taken up with practicing. Even if I had the money, I wouldn't go.' He looked at me curiously. 'You are devoted to mathematics the way I am to music, aren't you? I think I heard your mother say so.'
I nodded, grateful for these words. He considered our situations to be comparable, and he didn't think that a girl being interested in math was any stranger than a boy being interested in music."

What can you infer about Kim?

_____

_____

_____

Compare ideas with your classmates.

⬛⬛⬛⬛⬛⬛⬛⬛⬛

READING STRATEGY:
Asking Questions
See page 249.

8. **Group Work.** Follow the steps below to share ideas about the story.

   a. Work together to brainstorm a list of opinion-based questions about the story. (Opinion-based questions have no right or wrong answers.) Ask questions that really interest you and write them down.

   b. Choose the three questions that interest you most and write them on another piece of paper.

   c. Exchange questions with another group.

d. Discuss the other group's questions and take notes on your group's answers.

e. Read the questions and your group's answers aloud to the class.

9. **Group Work.** Share ideas about the story. Choose two questions from the list below to discuss in your group. Choose one person in your group to take notes.

> CRITICAL THINKING
> STRATEGY:
> *Interpreting*
> See page 262.

a. In what way does this story illustrate the ideas in the article by Landis on pages 48–49?

b. Do Emma's teachers fit the description of teachers in the article by Landis on pages 48–49? Why or why not?

c. Think back to the article *The Americanization of George* on pages 68–69. In what ways is Emma Hu becoming Americanized? How do you think her parents might react to this?

d. What does this story tell you about gender roles in the United States?

Tell your classmates which questions your group discussed. Briefly report your group's ideas.

10. **On your own.** Choose one character in the story. Write a sentence that gives your general impression of this character. Then give examples to support your idea.

> WRITING STRATEGY:
> *Giving Examples*
> See page 240.

Example:

General impression:	*Mr. Antonelli was a good teacher.*
Example:	*He didn't treat girls and boys differently.*

Share your ideas with the class.

CRITICAL THINKING
STRATEGY:
Synthesizing
See page 263.

WRITING STRATEGY:
Quickwriting
See page 246.

Listing Ideas
See page 241.

WRITING STRATEGY:
Organizing Ideas
See page 245.

11. **Writing Project.** In the article on pages 48–49, Judson Landis states that "the results of gender-role stereotyping are many and varied." Give your interpretation of this statement, using your experiences and observations as well as ideas from the readings in this unit. Here are some suggestions you can follow to help you get started:

a. In what ways has gender-role stereotyping affected your life? Quickwrite for five to ten minutes in your journal.

b. Look for examples of the effects of gender-role stereotying in the four readings in this unit. List these examples in your journal:

1. According to Judson Landis, how does gender-role stereotyping affect young children? (Chapter 1)

2. How does gender-role stereotyping affect professional women? (Chapter 2)

3. How does gender-role stereotyping affect George in the article *The Americanization of George?* (Chapter 3)

4. How does gender-role stereotyping affect Emma Hu in the short story *Who's Hu?* (Chapter 4)

c. Talk to a friend or classmate of the opposite gender. Find out how gender-role stereotyping has affected this person. Take notes on your conversation.

d. Look over your notes and your quickwriting. Choose the ideas that you want to include in your writing. Think about how you might organize your ideas.

e. Write a first draft of your paper.

f. Place a copy of your writing in your writing folder.

UNIT TWO
Final Project

You now have four pieces of writing from Unit Two in your writing folder, one from the writing assignment at the end of each chapter. Each is a rough draft—a collection of first ideas.

Choose one of these drafts to revise. It doesn't matter which one you choose, but you'll probably want to choose the one that interests you most. Before you start revising, though, read the notes below.

Notes on Revising

From your final project at the end of Unit One, you already know three reasons to revise:

- to sharpen your focus

- to make your writing interesting to your readers

- to help your readers follow your ideas

Before you start revising your first draft, though, think about how you can make your writing interesting to your readers.

☑ *Revising to make your writing interesting*

1. **Use your introduction to get your reader's attention.** Your introduction needs to be a "hook." Like a hook to catch a fish, a hook in writing catches readers and draws them into the writing.

   A quotation can be a hook. For example, you might begin an essay about learning gender roles with something a parent often said to you:

   "Always act like a lady," my mother said to me, whenever she thought I was talking too much or too loud. Both of my parents had firm ideas of how "ladies" were supposed to act.…

85

A startling detail or example can be a hook. For instance, you might begin an essay on gender stereotyping like this:

> *Recent research conducted in elementary school classrooms shows that teachers give more attention to boys than to girls... .*

A generalization that promises a full explanation can be a hook. For example, you might begin an essay on gender stereotyping like this:

> *"The results of gender-role stereotyping are many and varied," says Judson Landis, a sociologist... .*

2. **Use details, examples, and quotations to make your writing interesting.** Your readers want to "see" what you mean. For example, in *The Americanization of George,* the writer uses strong detail to describe his son's behavior:

   > *...George would interrupt his play and rush across the driveway to greet me; often, he would literally hurl himself into my open arms. (pg. 68)*

   Examples also hold your readers' attention. For instance, also in *The Americanization of George,* the writer promises an example to help readers follow George's shift to "Americanized" behavior:

   > *His "Americanization" was most forcefully conveyed by a recent incident on the tennis court. (pg. 69)*

   Quotations let your readers "hear" what you mean. For example, in the story *Who's Hu,* Arthur Aldrich's voice matches his arrogant behavior:

   > *"I can do better than you any day, don't you worry! But I know you're desperate to go to the prom, right." (pg. 78)*

3. **Let <u>your</u> voice as a writer come through to your readers.** Readers want to feel that a real, live person is communicating with them. Your voice can be formal or not-so-formal, happy or sad, strong or gentle, but it should be <u>real</u>. You can also change your voice from one piece of writing to the next.

Compare the voices of two different writers. One "speaks" as a competent professional; the other "speaks" as a concerned father:

> *…sex differences are socially learned and publicly performed but are relatively unconscious in both the sender and receiver—until someone breaks the rules or norms. (pg. 61)*

> *America is coming between me and my 12-year old son. (pg. 68)*

Your voice depends on you, your audience, and your purpose for writing.

We asked Amanda Buege, an experienced writer, to tell us what she does to make her writing interesting. Here's what she said:

Making Your Writing Interesting

Before I moved to New Orleans to study, my St. Louis friend Rod gave me a bit of advice about my writing. "Amanda," he said, "when you write, make sure your first sentence is a strong hook. That first sentence needs to grab your readers by the shirt collar and yell, 'Keep reading this story!'"

I remember wondering at the time whether Rod wasn't a little over-enthusiastic about first lines. But in the last two years of studying and writing, I've realized that Rod's advice makes sense. He wanted to grab me by my collar to make sure I was paying attention. I was Rod's audience, and he had something important to tell me. He hooked me, and I listened.

Because I seem to be writing all the time, I'm also revising all the time. For me, revising is central to my writing process. When I'm revising, I try to remember Rod's advice—as well as other revising tidbits[1] I've picked up. I don't just work by other writers' rules, though; I decide what advice works for *me*. Rereading my writing—again and again—works for me. Rewriting—again and again—works for me. Sometimes I throw out whole paragraphs, if they don't seem interesting enough. When I revise, I also add details, details, and more details.

Sometimes a certain section seems particularly dry, without any real voice behind it. Then I try to reintroduce my "personality." After all, *I* am the author, and my voice should come through loud and clear.

I've also discovered that my first sentence doesn't always need to shout and

---

1 **tidbits**   the very best little pieces (of food, gossip, etc.)

grab, as Rod suggested. Sometimes, it can whisper instead—simply hinting[2] at all the good reading to come.

—Amanda Buege

---

2 **hinting**   suggesting, without telling directly

Process of Revising

As you start revising your first draft, here are some suggestions:

❖ **Writing a second draft.** Use the revising checklist on the next page to evaluate your first draft. Decide what changes you want to make and make notes in the margin of your paper. When you are ready, work from your notes and write a new draft.

❖ **Writing a third draft.** Ask a classmate to read your second draft and complete the revising checklist. From your classmate's evaluation and your own ideas, decide what changes you want to make and note them in the margin of your paper. When you are ready, write a new draft.

❖ **Writing additional drafts.** Repeat any part of the process until you are satisfied with your writing. Your teacher may want to use the checklist to evaluate your final draft.

Unit Two
Revising Checklist

Yes ✓

Sharpening your focus	First draft	Second draft	Third draft	Final draft
• Is it clear who the audience is?	❑	❑	❑	❑
• Is the topic limited enough?	❑	❑	❑	❑
• Have unnecessary words been deleted?	❑	❑	❑	❑
Making your writing interesting				
• Does the introduction "hook" the reader?	❑	❑	❑	❑
• Does the writer use interesting details?	❑	❑	❑	❑
• Does the writer's voice come through?	❑	❑	❑	❑

Your final draft may be placed in a class booklet, along with your classmates' writing. You can pass the booklet around for everyone to read.

UNIT THREE
Working for Social and Political Change

In this unit you will read four selections related to the theme of social and political change.

- What are some of the important social and political changes that have taken place in the last 50 years?
- Where have these changes taken place?
- What caused these changes to take place?
- What are some ways that people can bring about social and political change?

CHAPTER ONE

Nonviolent Resistance

1. **Group Work.** *Nonviolent resistance* is a strategy for achieving political and social change. How could you further define this term? What examples can you give to illustrate your definition? Write your group's ideas on the lines below.

   Our definition:

   _____

   _____

   _____

   Examples:

   _____

   _____

   _____

   _____

   Share your group's ideas with the class.

CRITICAL THINKING STRATEGY:
Applying What You Know
See page 259.

---

2. **Group Work.** Plan a scene to illustrate *nonviolent resistance*. On separate paper, write out a *script* (what the "actors" do and say). Then rehearse the scene and perform it for the class.

   Afterwards, as a class, tell how each group's performance illustrates *nonviolent resistance*.

3. **Class Work.** The article on pages 94–96 is an excerpt from a text-book called *Introduction to Peace Studies.* Read the title and first paragraph of this article and then answer the questions at the top of the chart below. Use information from the paragraph and from the collective knowledge of the class to come up with ideas. Record the ideas below, so that everyone will have a list.

READING STRATEGY:
Previewing
See page 253.

What do you know about Mohandas Gandhi?	**What do you want to find out about Mohandas Gandhi?**
He was from India.	*What impact did his teaching have?*

4. **On your own.** Read the whole article on pages 94–96. As you read, look for answers to questions about Gandhi from Activity 3. As you come across an idea that will help you answer a question, make a note in the margin. Then you can locate the idea later.

READING STRATEGY:
Reading for Specific Information
See page 254.

Writing Margin Notes
See page 257.

Mohandas K. Gandhi

by David P. Barash

from *Introduction to Peace Studies,* a textbook

Mohandas Gandhi is revered by Indians as the founder of their nation, 1
and also by millions of others as the leading exponent[1] of nonviolence. He
pioneered the use of nonviolent resistance as both a spiritual and philo-
sophical approach to life and an intensely practical technique of achieving
political and social change. Gandhi was widely known among Indians as
"Mahatma" (Great Soul), for his courage, simplicity, and penetrating
insight, and for the extraordinary impact[2] of his teachings and his life.

Central to Gandhi's world view was the search for truth, and indeed, he 2
titled his autobiography *My Experiments with Truth.* Gandhi considered that
truth (*ahimsa,* in Sanskrit) was achievable only through love and tolerance
for other people; moreover, it required continual testing, experimentation,
occasional errors, and constant, unstinting[3] effort. His teachings empha-
sized courage, directness, friendly civility, absolute honesty, nonviolence to
all living creatures, and adherence[4] to the truth. Perhaps the most important
Gandhian concept is *satyagraha,* literally translated as "soul-force" or
"soul-truth." *Satyagraha* requires a clearheaded adherence to goals of love
and mutual respect, and it demands a willingness to suffer, if need be, to
achieve these goals.

Early Years

Gandhi was born in India, in 1869; his parents were merchant-caste[5] 3
Hindus. He remained a devout Hindu throughout his life, although his
thinking incorporated elements from numerous other religious and ethical
traditions. He was strongly influenced by pacifist[6] Christianity, as well as
by the writings of Thoreau and Tolstoy on the rights and duties of individ-

---

1 **exponent**   champion
2 **impact**   influence
3 **unstinting**   limitless
4 **adherence**   support, loyalty
5 **caste**   social class a person is born into
6 **pacifist**   peace-loving, anti-war

Gandhi addresses prayer meeting in New Delhi on January 14, 1948.

uals to practice civil disobedience[7] when governmental authorities are insensitive to higher morality. He married very young (he and his wife were both 13), and studied law in London. After a brief time in India, the young barrister[8] went to South Africa, where he was outraged by that country's system of racial discrimination (there was, and still is, a large Asian—especially Indian—population in South Africa). He remained there for twenty-one years, leading numerous campaigns for Indian rights, editing a newspaper, and developing his philosophy of nonviolent action as well as specific techniques for implementing it. He was physically abused and arrested many times by British authorities, but also served courageously on the British side when he agreed with their positions; for example, he organized an Indian Ambulance Corps during the Boer War (1899–1902) and the Zulu Rebellion (1906), for which he was decorated[9] by the government.

---

7 **civil disobedience**　refusing to obey the government in order to force the government to change

8 **barrister**　courtroom lawyer

9 **decorated**　given an honor

Gandhi.

Return to India

After achieving some notable reforms, Gandhi returned to India in   4
1915, and within a few years became the leader of the Indian nationalist
movement, seeking independence from colonial Britain. When the British
government made it illegal to organize political opposition, Gandhi led a
successful *satyagraha*[10] campaign against these laws. In 1919, British troops
fired into a crowd of unarmed Indian men, women, and children, who had
been demonstrating peacefully; nearly 400 were killed in what became
known as the Amritsar Massacre. This slaughter served to highlight[11] the
difference between the steadfast nonviolence of Gandhi's followers and the
relative brutality of the colonial government; it also moved Gandhi to refine
and further develop his techniques of *satyagraha.* In particular, he took
the great Hindu war epic,[12] the *Bhagavad-Gita,* to be an allegory[13] not about
war, but about the human soul, and the need for all people to devote themselves, unselfishly, to the attainment of their goals. He urged that for real
success, it is necessary to "reduce yourself to zero," that is, to remove the

10 *satyagraha*   a Hindi word for passive resistance and nonviolence
11 **highlight**   direct attention to
12 **epic**   long poem telling historical events
13 **allegory**   a symbolic story

self-will and striving for personal aggrandizement[14] that so often leads to arrogance or even tyranny.

5   Gandhi frequently employed fasts[15] to emphasize the importance of personal suffering and to protest the violence that periodically broke out, as less disciplined Indian nationalists rioted against British rule, notably during the Bombay riots in 1921 and the Chauri-Chaura riots in 1922. Following these painful experiences, Gandhi temporarily called off his struggle for Indian independence. During the 1920s, Gandhi continued to fight for the rights of the lowest Hindu caste, the Untouchables—whom he renamed the *Harijan* (children of God)—and for miners, factory workers, and poor peasants. He urged Indians to develop cottage industries, such as spinning and weaving, so as to deprive Great Britain of its major economic advantage in occupying India: markets for English textile products. Hand weaving contributed to the potential of Indian national self-sufficiency, while also emphasizing the dignity of labor.

6   When Britain introduced the Salt Acts, requiring that all salt must be purchased from the government, Gandhi led a massive march, 320 kilometers to the sea, where he and his followers made salt from seawater, in defiance of the law. In all, Gandhi spent about seven years in various jails for his numerous acts of nonviolent resistance, making it respectable—indeed, honorable—for protesters to be imprisoned for their beliefs. He was a small, slight man with indomitable moral certitude[16] and remarkable physical stamina. He was an ascetic[17] and intensely frugal,[18] and he also possessed a biting sense of humor; once, when he visited the British king in London, the half-naked Gandhi was asked whether he felt a bit underdressed for the occasion, to which he replied, "His Majesty wore enough for two of us." Another time, when asked what he thought of Western civilization, he replied, "I think it would be a good idea."

7   Gandhi was deeply grieved by the intense periodic violence between Hindus and Moslems, and he opposed the partition of British colonial India into an independent Moslem Pakistan and Hindu India. He was assassinated (by a high-ranking Hindu who opposed his insistence on religious tolerance) in 1948, the year after India won its independence from Britain. However, Gandhi accomplished what many thought impossible: He led his country of 400 million people to freedom without firing a shot. He also showed that a highly spiritual concept—nonviolence—can be an intensely practical tool in the quest for peace, even in the twentieth-century world of *realpolitik*,[19] power, and violence.

---

14 **aggrandizement**   greater importance
15 **fasts**   eating no food
16 **certitude**   feeling of absolute sureness
17 **ascetic**   person who lives simply in order to achieve a greater spiritual level
18 **frugal**   thrifty, economical, not wasteful
19 *realpolitik*   practical politics, not theory

READING STRATEGY:
Finding Main Ideas
See page 250.

5. Class Work. Share answers you found to the questions from Activity 3. If your classmates found an answer that you didn't find, make a note in the margin next to the idea in the reading.

Then, on your own, read the article again. As you read a second time, underline any other ideas that you think are important.

READING STRATEGY:
Using Context
See page 255.

6. On your own. Choose five words that were unfamiliar to you when you first read the Gandhi article. List them below. Which of these words were you able to define, using context? Write your definitions in the chart. Then look up these words in a dictionary to check your guesses.

Words	My definition from context	Dictionary definition

Share what you learned with your classmates.

READING STRATEGY:
Making a Time Line
See page 251.

7. On your own. On another piece of paper, make a time line showing the important events in the life of Mohandas Gandhi.

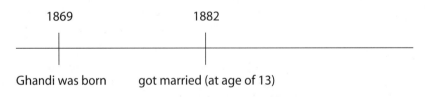

1869	1882
Ghandi was born	got married (at age of 13)

Get together with a partner. Without looking at your partner's time line, compare ideas.

8. Pair Work. The sentences below are from the Gandhi article on pages 94–96. Based on the information in these sentences, what inferences can you make?

READING STRATEGY:
Making Inferences
See page 252.

a. "He [Gandhi] remained a devout Hindu throughout his life, although his thinking incorporated elements from numerous other religious and ethical traditions."

What can you infer about Gandhi?

_____

_____

b. "He [Gandhi] married very young (he and his wife were both 13) and studied law in London."

What can you infer about Gandhi's parents?

_____

_____

c. "…[Gandhi] went to South Africa, where he was outraged by the country's system of racial discrimination… ."

What can you infer about Gandhi?

_____

_____

d. "He [Gandhi] was physically abused and arrested many times by British authorities [in South Africa], but also served courageously on the British side when he agreed with their positions… ."

What can you infer about Gandhi?

_____

_____

e. "During the 1920s, [in India] Gandhi continued to fight for the rights of the lowest Hindu caste…and for miners, factory workers, and poor peasants."

What can you infer about Gandhi?

_____

_____

f. "…when asked what he thought of Western civilization, he [Gandhi] replied, 'I think it would be a good idea.'"

What can you infer about Gandhi?

_____

_____

When you finish, get together with two other classmates and share ideas.

WRITING STRATEGY:
Quickwriting
See page 246.

9. **On your own.** Look back at the definition and examples of *nonviolent resistance* in Activity 1. What further ideas do you have? In your journal, write down ideas that come to mind. Try to write for five minutes without stopping. The questions below may help you get started.

• What does nonviolent resistance, as an idea, mean to you?

• Is nonviolent resistance an effective instrument of change? Why or why not?

• What examples support your thinking?

10. **Writing Project.** Choose a descriptive word or phrase that applies to Gandhi, for example, *courageous* or *dedicated.* Explore your definition of this word or phrase, and then show how this word applies to Gandhi. Here are some suggestions to help you get started.

WRITING STRATEGY:
Making a Tree Diagram
See page 244.

a. Look back over the reading to find words and ideas that describe Gandhi. Write them on a tree diagram.

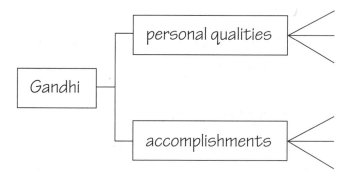

b. Look over your tree diagram and choose a word or phrase that interests you. Quickwrite about it for five to ten minutes.

Example:

What does it mean to be courageous? It's not the same as being fearless. You aren't being courageous if you don't feel threatened in some way... .

c. Look back over your quickwriting. Circle ideas you might want to use in your writing. Also look back over the Gandhi article and your margin notes. Make notes in your journal of ideas you might use. Write down words or whole quotations that might help you explain your ideas. Be sure to give the author, David Baresh, credit.

Example:

To support the claim that Gandhi was, by nature, peace-loving, you might cite the following idea from Baresh's article:

"Gandhi was grieved by the violence between Hindus and Moslems in British colonial India, according to David Baresh in *Introduction to Peace Studies.*"

d. Decide who your audience is. Is your reader someone who knows nothing about Gandhi? Someone who thinks violence is the best way to settle disputes? Peace-loving people? Identify the audience you plan to keep in mind as you write.

WRITING STRATEGY:
Quickwriting
See page 246.

WRITING STRATEGY:
Collecting Information
See page 238.

Citing Sources
See page 237.

WRITING STRATEGY:
Understanding Your Audience
See page 247.

My probable audience:

_____

What do you want your audience to know or do? Write down your goals below.

What I want my audience to know or do:

_____

_____

_____

e. Drawing from your notes, journal writing, and other work, write a first draft of your paper.

f. After you finish your first draft, ask a classmate to read it. What questions does your classmate have? From your classmate's questions, make notes in the margin of your draft for future work.

g. Place a copy of your draft in your writing folder.

CHAPTER TWO

Would You Have the Courage to Say No?

1. **Class Work.** Read the title of the magazine article on page 105. When might someone say this? Under what circumstances? Share your ideas with your classmates.

2. **Group Work.** Study the photographs and read the captions on pages 103–104. Then answer the question on page 104.

CRITICAL THINKING STRATEGY:
Interpreting
See page 262.

Synthesizing
See page 263.

In the 1950s, black people living in the South were segregated, or separated, from white people. Laws required separate facilities—schools, movie theaters, drinking fountains, swimming pools, libraries, churches, parks—for blacks and whites. Usually, the facilities for blacks were inferior in quality.

In some cities, black people had to sit in the back of city buses. On a crowded bus, black people had to get up and give their seats to white people.

On December l, 1955, Rosa Parks refused to get up and give her seat to a white person. For this action, she was taken to jail and fined. In response, the black people of Montgomery, Alabama, decided to boycott the city buses. The boycott lasted more than a year, until the Supreme Court of the United States ruled that segregation on city buses was illegal. For many people, the Montogomery Bus Boycott marked the beginning of the modern civil rights movement.

Question: If you were assigned to interview Rosa Parks today, what questions would you ask her?

Choose one person to write down your group's questions. Then read your questions aloud to the class and make a master list on the board. Before the master list gets erased, copy it into your journal, leaving space to write answers.

READING STRATEGY:
Reading for Specific Information
See page 254.

3. **On your own.** Read the article on pages 105–108. As you read, underline information that may help you to answer the questions from Activity 2. When you finish, write in any answers that you found.

I Wanted To Be Treated Like a Human Being

by Marie Ragghianti

from *Parade Magazine*

1   I first met Rosa Parks in New York City in 1986 at a high-powered gathering of feminist and political leaders. My impression remains vivid. She was poised, even regal, yet there was a distinct modesty and an aura of spirituality about her.

2   Thirty-six years ago, on a bus in Montgomery, Alabama, Rosa Parks refused to give up her seat to a white man, defying a Southern tradition of decades. To appreciate that act we have to remember that the mid-1950s were a time when the Ku Klux Klan[1] was in its heyday,[2] when the 1954 Supreme Court ruling against segregation in the schools had fanned the bigotry of white supremacists,[3] and when lynchings[4] of blacks in the Deep South were being widely reported. If the precise moment of the birth of the Civil Rights movement can be isolated, it may be said that it was from this one woman's singular act of courage.

3   As an adolescent, my youthful ideal-ism[5] had been fired when I read about Rosa Parks. Our brief introduction that evening in 1986 rekindled my imagination: Who was Rosa Parks, really? Who was she then? Who is she now? How could someone so apparently shy have been bold enough to challenge a whole system embedded in racism? Was she a figurehead for the Civil Rights movement—perhaps, as some have argued, only a plant[6] for the NAACP,[7] someone whose act was part of a master plan designed to foster a call for the desegregation of public transportation? Or was she the authentic heroine of my youth? I wanted to find out for myself.

4   My search finally ended late last year in Detroit. It had not been easy to find her, and it was even harder to fit into her schedule. At the age of 78, Rosa Parks maintains a level of activity that would daunt[8] someone half her age. We met out-

---

1 **Ku Klux Klan**   secret group dedicated to the belief in the superiority of white people
2 **heyday**   time of greatest success or prosperity
3 **white supremacists**   white people who believe that whites are superior to other races
4 **lynchings**   murders of suspected criminals by mob action, usually by hanging
5 **idealism**   belief in a more perfect world
6 **plant**   spy
7 **NAACP**   National Association for the Advancement of Colored People, a civil rights organization
8 **daunt**   discourage

Rosa Parks being fingerprinted after her 1955 arrest in Montgomery, Alabama.

tary of the city's branch of the NAACP], and I was preparing for the weekend workshop for the Youth Council."

8 She turned slightly, and an almost wistful expression crossed her face. Then, I was startled by a revelation[10] that she offered almost offhandedly. Suddenly, she was talking about another day, another time, another bus—but the same driver.

9 "The same driver, back in 1943, had evicted me"[11] from the bus," she said. "It was not about a seat that time. He wanted me to get off the bus and go around and get back on. I wouldn't do it."

10 In those days in the South, black people were expected to board the front of the bus, pay their fare, then get off and walk outside the bus to reboard on the back. But the back already was crowded, she explained—standing room only—and she couldn't help but notice that black passengers were standing even on the back steps of the vehicle. It was apparent that it would be all but impossible to reboard at the back. Besides, it was no secret that bus drivers sometimes drove off and left black passengers behind, even after accepting their fares. Rosa Parks spontaneously decided to take her chances. She paid her fare in the front of the bus, then walked down the aisle, hoping to unobtrusively find a spot as close to the back as she could get.

11 "When he saw what I was doing," she said, "he got up and ordered me to get off

side a church where she was appearing and the voices of children filled the air.

5 I was struck by the curious blend of seeming contradictions that she presented. She is grandmotherly in appearance, her hair a silvery crown, yet she retains the grace of a young woman. Rather than the imposing physical presence that one might expect, she is petite and slim. And she is soft-spoken—so soft-spoken that one must lean toward her to hear her words.

6 I asked her about that fateful day, a Thursday. Had she known when she got up that morning what lay ahead?[9] Had there been a plan?

7 "I wasn't planning to be arrested at all," she said. "I would rather not have been arrested, of course. I had a full weekend planned. It was December, Christmastime. It was the busy time of year [she was a tailor's assistant in a men's clothing store in Montgomery and secre-

---

9 **lay ahead**   was in the future

10 **revelation**   surprising information
11 **evicted me**   forced me to leave

Rosa Parks in a recent photo.

the bus. He wanted me to go around to the back door and get back on. When I refused, he came back and grabbed my coat sleeve—not my arm, just the sleeve. I didn't really resist at that point. But I wasn't going to get off and go around. My purse fell, and one or two things fell out. I picked them up, even though I was afraid he would attack me physically. He was livid with anger."[12]

12   She was evicted from the bus that day but not arrested. For 12 years, she never forgot what that driver looked like. "I saw him occasionally when I was waiting for the bus," she said, "but I didn't ride the bus if he was driving." But on Dec. 1, 1955, she was in a hurry. She had a lot of things to get done. When the bus came, she got on without paying attention to the driver.

13   It is clear that what happened next was not part of a preplanned strategy. "I had had enough," she stated simply. "I wanted to be treated like a human being."

14   The bus already was crowded when she boarded. "There was a [black] man sitting next to the window," she recalled. "I sat next to him. There were two [black] women across the aisle. We went through one stop without being disturbed. But at the second stop, a [white] man got on and had to stand. He was not saying anything at all, not a word, but the bus driver noticed him." Immediately, the driver ordered the four black passengers to surrender their seats so the white man could sit down. The man beside Rosa Parks stood up after the driver spoke a second time.

15   "The driver said, 'Y'all make it light on yourselves,'" she remembered. "The two women moved then, but I moved next to the window. He asked me to move. I said, 'No.' Several people [all black] got off the bus." She does not comment on the obvious: Only the black passengers were fearful of what might happen next.

16   "When the [two] policemen came on the bus and wanted to know what was wrong, the driver pointed to me and said, 'That one won't stand up.' I asked, 'Why do you all treat us this way?' One of the policemen said, 'I don't know—the law is the law.'"

17   "I stood up. One took my purse, the other my shopping bag. I got in the back of the police car." She was taken to City Hall, booked,[13] fingerprinted, jailed and

---

12 **livid with anger**   very angry, furious

13 **booked**   charges against her were recorded by the police

fined. Her arrest and subsequent appeal were the catalyst for a yearlong boycott[14] of the city's buses by blacks, who made up 70 percent of their riders. The boycott, which brought Martin Luther King Jr. to national prominence, ended when a Supreme Court order declared Montgomery's segregated seating laws unconstitutional.

18   Fred Gray, who defended Rosa Parks at the time, is still practicing law in Tuskegee, Ala. I asked him what it was like to represent her. "Mrs. Parks was very easy-going and cooperative," he recalled. "She was a lovely person to work with."

19   I had been unable to shake my impression of her as shy, and I asked whether he agreed. "Reserved," he said. "Not really shy. She's forceful."

20   Little has been written about Rosa Parks' life outside of the bus boycott. Her husband, Raymond Parks, was an activist at a time when to be one was to invite danger. He was in the vanguard[15] of those who fought for the release and vindication[16] of the Scottsboro Boys, nine black youths convicted on trumped-up[17] charges of raping a white woman in 1931. He and Rosa were married in 1931, and he encouraged her to become involved in the NAACP in the early '40s.

21   Although they never had children, Rosa Parks always has been committed to children. Today, she spends much of her time at the Rosa and Raymond Parks Institute for Self Development. Founded in Detroit in 1987, the institute is a non-profit foundation that focuses on the "average" child, the one who often comes out on the short end[18] of social programs. Mrs. Parks and the institute's board members believe it is the average child who may profit most from the lessons of history and from programs designed to foster[19] awareness and involvement. The institute also provides scholarships for youths.

22   Perhaps the most unusual of the many programs the institute offers (co-sponsored with other Michigan groups) is the Reverse Freedom Tour, an annual event that brings together teenagers from the Deep South and the North and takes them by bus on a cross-country trip that retraces major landmarks of Civil Rights history— including the site in Montgomery where Rosa Parks refused to get off the bus. The tour's highlight is a retracing of the Underground Railroad, the route of escaped slaves, both in the U.S. and Canada.

Tamica Mingo, 17, whose dream is to work in television, recalled how Rosa Parks had joined them on the Reverse Freedom Tour. "She never got tired of us," Tamica said. "She was willing to answer all the questions we had."

"Even now, " Tamica added, "Mrs. Parks doesn't think of herself as a heroine. She did it because it was right. She doesn't see herself as the Mother of the Civil Rights movement, but I see her as that. All children do."

---

14 **boycott**   organized refusal to use or buy something
15 **vanguard**   leadership
16 **vindication**   clearing of blame
17 **trumped-up**   false, untrue
18 **comes out on the short end**   loses, is in a losing position
19 **foster**   promote, push for

4. **Class Work.** Share any answers that you found to the questions from Activity 2. Then read the article again. As you read a second time, write your thoughts and questions in the margin.

READING STRATEGY:
Writing Margin Notes
See page 257.

Using Context
See page 255.

5. **On your own.** Find the *italicized* words below in the reading. Use context to guess the meaning of each one. Then give examples to "show" what the words mean. After you finish, compare guesses and examples with your classmates.

   a. Paragraph #3: *bold*

   My guess: _____

   Example of a <u>bold</u> action:

   _____

   b. Paragraph #5: *contradiction*

   My guess: _____

   Example of a <u>contradiction</u>:

   _____

   c. Paragraph #5: *imposing*

   My guess: _____

   Description of someone with an <u>imposing</u> physical presence:

   _____

   d. Paragraph #10: *unobtrusively*

   My guess: _____

   Example of how you could enter a room <u>unobtrusively</u>:

   _____

e. Paragraph #17: *catalyst*

My guess: _____

Example of a possible <u>catalyst</u> for war:

_____

CRITICAL THINKING STRATEGY:
Applying What You Know
See page 259.

6. **Group Work.** In the article, Rosa Parks describes two instances when the same driver evicted her from the bus—once in 1943 and again in 1955. Using information from the article, choose one of the occasions and plan how your group will act it out. On separate paper, write a script (what the "actors" do and say). Rehearse it and then perform it for the class.

READING STRATEGY:
Making a Tree Diagram
See page 252.

7. **On your own.** How would you describe Rosa Parks? Add information from the article to the tree diagram below.

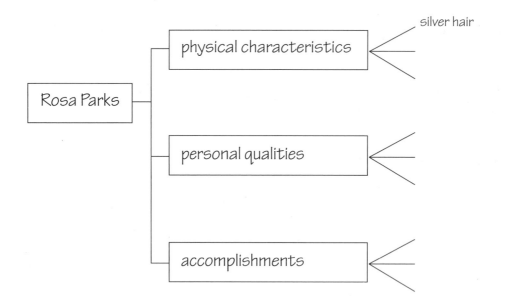

After you finish, compare diagrams with a partner. Help each other complete the diagram, if one of you has information the other missed.

8. **Pair Work.** Write three opinion questions based on the article. (*Opinion questions* do not have right or wrong answers; they ask for someone's opinion.)

   Example:

   Do you think Rosa Parks was courageous? Why or why not?

   Exchange questions with two other classmates and answer their questions. Be sure to give reasons and/or examples to support your answers. Record your answers, and then read them to the class.

9. **On your own.** Choose a statement or event from the Rosa Parks article that interests you. In your journal, write about it for five to ten minutes without stopping. The questions below might help you get started:

   • What does this statement or event remind you of?

   • How does your own experience relate to it?

   • What, in your opinion, is its importance?

   After you finish, tell a classmate about an idea from your journal writing.

10. **On your own.** Look back at the ideas you underlined in the article. Also check your margin notes. On separate paper, then write a summary, including only the ideas that you think are most basic to understanding the article.

    After you finish, exchange summaries with a classmate. Compare ideas. Did your partner think different ideas were important? If there are differences, explain why you included the ideas you did.

READING STRATEGY:
Distinguishing Fact and Opinion
See page 249.

CRITICAL THINKING STRATEGY:
Synthesizing
See page 263.

READING STRATEGY:
Summarizing
See page 254.

---

11. **Writing Project.** Both Mohandas Gandhi and Rosa Parks were activists. *(Activists* are individuals who act to bring about social and/or political change.) In writing, explore their similarities. Here are some suggestions to help you get started.

▓▓░▓◇▓▓░▓◇▓▓░▓◇▓▓░▓◇▓

WRITING STRATEGY:
Quickwriting
See page 246.

a. In your journal, quickwrite about Mohandas Gandhi for five minutes.

   • What did Gandhi do?

   • What is remarkable about what he did?

   • What changes did he bring about?

   • What lessons can we learn from his actions?

b. Quickwrite about Rosa Parks. Think about the same questions.

▓▓░▓◇▓▓░▓◇▓▓░▓◇▓▓░▓◇▓

WRITING STRATEGY:
Focusing Your Ideas
See page 239.

c. Look over your quickwriting and choose one or two points of similarity to focus on. Choose a focus that is important to you and note it below.

Possible focus for my writing:

_____

_____

_____

▓▓░▓◇▓▓░▓◇▓▓░▓◇▓▓░▓◇▓

WRITING STRATEGY:
Collecting Information
See page 238.

d. Look through your journal writing and through the readings on Gandhi and Parks for ideas, words, and quotations that you might use in your paper. Make notes in your journal: use your journal as a "storehouse" of ideas.

e. Imagine an audience for your paper. Think about who needs to understand what you have to say: Leaders of oppressive governments? Citizens who ignore the rights of others? A young person who might become a Mohandas Gandhi or a Rosa Parks some day? Someone else? Write down who you think your audience is.

Possible audience:

_____

f. Think about how best to "reach" your audience: A newspaper article? A public address (speech)? A dialogue between Gandhi and Parks? Some other way?

g. Drawing from your notes, write a first draft.

h. After you finish your draft, ask a classmate to read it. Does your classmate have any questions? From these questions, make notes in the margin of your draft for future work.

i. Place your draft in your writing folder.

> **WRITING STRATEGY:**
> *Understanding Your Audience*
> See page 247.

CHAPTER THREE

Save a Village, Save the World

CRITICAL THINKING STRATEGY: *Classifying* See page 260.

1. **Class Work.** What are some of the most important problems of our time? Brainstorm ideas and make a list on the board. After you finish listing ideas, identify which problems are *local* (in the town or city where you live) and which are *global* (in scattered places all over the world). Some might be both.

Problems	Local/Global
water pollution	*L, G*
human rights abuses	*G*

CRITICAL THINKING STRATEGY: *Analyzing* See page 258.

2. **On your own.** Choose what you think is the most important problem on the list and write about it in your journal for five minutes. Here are some suggestions to help you get started.

   • What do you know about this problem?

   • Why do you think it is so important?

   • What are some solutions to this problem?

   • Are people working on this problem? If so, who?

   Choose an idea from your journal writing to share with the class.

3. **Group Work.** In Activity 1, you thought about things that need to be changed. Now, think about individuals who have worked to bring about change. These people don't need to be famous for you to add them to the list on the next page.

Who	Person's action	Change (actual or potential)
Rosa Parks	refused to give up her seat on the bus	desegregated public transportation in Montgomery, Alabama

When you finish, share information about a person from your list with the class.

4. **On your own.** Read the title of the magazine article on page 116 and the italicized information following the title. Then write five questions that you think will be answered in the article.

READING STRATEGY:
Predicting
See page 253.

Questions	Answers
Example:	
Why did Paiakan have to leave his village	
to save it?	
1.	
2.	
3.	
4.	
5.	

After you finish, read the whole article on pages 116–119 and underline information that you think answers your questions.

"I Fight for Our Future"

by Hank Whittemore

from *Parade Magazine*

Several years ago, a young Kayapo Indian named Paulo Paiakan left his village in the Amazon rain forest of Brazil in order to save it. He ventured to the outside world, warning that if the forest disappears, his people will die. Today he is still standing against the forces of destruction as time runs out. At stake[1] is far more than the fate of a remote Kayapo village. The rain forest is one of the world's great biological treasures. If the Kayapo lose the forest that sustains[2] their life, so will we.

1 …Among the Kayapo, preparation for a new leader begins at birth. Such was the case for Paiakan, who is descended from a long line of chiefs. His father is a highly regarded peacemaker; and when Paiakan was born, the tribe received a "vision" of his special destiny.

2 "When I was still a boy," Paiakan recalls, "I knew that one day I would go into the world to learn what was coming to us."

3 As a teenager, Paiakan got his chance. He was sent to the Kayapo village of Gorotire for missionary school, where he met white men who were building the Trans-Amazonian Highway through the jungle. Paiakan was recruited to go out ahead of the road's progress, to approach the previously uncontacted tribes.

4 When he went back to see what was coming on the road, however, he saw an invasion of ranchers, miners and loggers using fires and chainsaws.[3] As he watched them tearing down vast tracts of forest and polluting the rivers with mercury, he realized that his actual job was to "pacify" other Indians into accepting it.

5 "I stopped working for the white man," he says, "and went back to my village. I told my people, 'They are cutting down the trees with big machines. They are killing the land and spoiling the river. They are great animals bringing great problems for us.' I told them we must leave, to get away from the threats."

6 Most of the Kayapo villagers did not believe him, arguing that the forest

---

1 **at stake**   at risk, in danger
2 **sustains**   supports
3 **chainsaw**   power tool for cutting down trees

The Amazon.

was indestructible.[4] So Paiakan formed a splinter group[5] of about 150 men, women, and children who agreed to move farther away. For the next two years, advance parties went ahead to plant crops and build homes. In 1983, they traveled four days together, 180 miles downriver, and settled in Aukre.

7   "Our life is better here," Paiakan says, "because this place is very rich in fish and game, with good soil. Our real name is *Mebengokre*—'people of the water's source.' The river is life for the plants and animals, as well as for the Indian."

8   But the new security did not last. During the 1980s, most other Kayapo villages in the Amazon were severely affected by the relentless invasions.[6] Along with polluted air and water came outbreaks of new diseases, requiring modern medicines for treatment. Aukre was still safe, but smoke from burning forests already could be seen and smelled. Paiakan, realizing that he could not run forever, made a courageous decision. He would leave his people again—this time, to go fight for them.

---

4 **indestructible**   not able to be destroyed
5 **splinter group**   small group that leaves the parent group
6 **relentless invasions**   forces entering continuously

Paulo Paiakan addresses tribal leaders and rain forest activists in Brazil.

He went to Belém, the state capital, where he learned to live, dress, and act like a white man. He learned to speak Portuguese, in order to communicate with government officials. He even taught himself to use a video camera, to document[7] the destruction of the forest—so his people could see it for themselves and so the Kayapo children would know about it.

Paiakan continued to travel between Aukre and the modern world, at one point becoming a government advisor on indigenous affairs[8] for the Amazon. In 1988, when the rubber tapper Chico Mendes was shot dead by ranchers for organizing grass-roots[9] resistance to deforestation, it was feared that Paiakan himself might be a target.

"Many indigenous leaders have been killed," says Darrell Posey, an ethnobiologist from the United States who has worked with the Indians of Brazil for 15 years, "but publicity surrounding the Mendes murder may

---

7 **document**   record
8 **indigenous affairs**   business of native people
9 **grass-roots**   at the local level

have helped to protect Paiakan." The Brazilian Pastoral Commission for Land has counted more than 1200 murders of activist peasants, union leaders, priests, and lawyers in the past decade.

12 In 1988, after speaking out against a proposed hydroelectric dam in the rain forest, both Paiakan and Posey were charged with breaking a Brazilian law against "foreigners" criticizing the government. Because Indians are not legally citizens, Paiakan faced three years in prison and expulsion from the country; but when other Kayapo learned of his plight,[10] some 400 leaders emerged from the forest in warpaint. The charges were dropped.

13 "In the old days," Paiakan told the press, "my people were great warriors. We were afraid of nothing. We are still not afraid of anything. But now, instead of war clubs, we are using words. And I had to come out, to tell you that by destroying our environment, you're destroying your own. If I didn't come out, you wouldn't know what you're doing."

14 In 1989, Paiakan organized an historic gathering in Altamira, Brazil, that brought together Indians and members of the environmental movement. A major theme of the conference was that protecting natural resources involves using the traditional knowledge of the indigenous peoples. "If you want to save the rain forest," he said, "you have to take into account[11] the people living there."

15 With increasing support, Paiakan acquired a small plane for flying to and from his village. He also made trips to the United States, Europe, and Japan, even touring briefly with the rock star Sting, to make speeches about the growing urgency of his people's plight.

16 But the erosion[12] of Indian culture in the Amazon forest was becoming pervasive.[13] With the influx of goods ranging from medicines to flashlights to radios to refrigerators to hunting gear, village after village was succumbing to internal pressure for money to buy more. By 1990, only Aukre and one other Kayapo community had refused to sell their tree-cutting rights to the loggers,[14] whose tactics included seductive offers of material goods to Indian leaders.

17 In June that year, racing against time, Paiakan completed negotiations for Aukre to make its own money while preserving the forest. Working with The Body Shop, an organic-cosmetic chain based in Britain, he arranged for villagers to harvest Brazil nuts and then create a natural oil to be used in hair conditioners. It would be their first product to export.

---

10 **plight** dangerous situation
11 **take into account** consider
12 **erosion** breaking down
13 **pervasive** present everywhere
14 **loggers** people who cut logs (trees)

Paiakan returned with his triumphant news only to learn that other 18 leaders of Aukre—during the previous month, in his absence—had sold the village's timber rights[15] for two years. It was a crushing blow, causing him to exclaim that all his "talking to the world" had been in vain.[16] He said that if he could not save his people, he would rather not live.

"He went through a period of intense, deep pain," says Saulo Petian, a 19 Brazilian from São Paulo employed by The Body Shop to work with the Kayapo. "He left the village and went far along the river, to be by himself. After about two months, when he got over his sadness and resentment, he came back and told me, 'Well, I traveled around the world and seemed to be successful, but the concrete results for the village were very little. These are my people. They have many needs. I can't go against them now.'"

So Paiakan made peace with the other leaders of his village and started 20 over. "I was like a man running along who got tired and stopped to rest," Paiakan recalls. "Then I came back, to continue my fight into the future."

What began was the simultaneous unfolding[17] of two events, by oppos- 21 ing forces, in Paiakan's village. One was the beginning of construction by the Indians of a small "factory" with a palm-leaf roof for creation of the hair-conditioning oil. For Paiakan, it was a way of showing his people how to earn money from the forest without allowing it to be destroyed. Meanwhile, loggers came through the forest constructing a road that skirted the edge of the village. By 1991, trucks were arriving from the frontier to carry back loads of freshly cut timber.

The white men left behind the first outbreak of malaria that Aukre had 22 seen, mainly afflicting[18] the elders and children. The only consolation for Paiakan was that the tree-cutters had just a couple of dry months each year when the road was passable.

"Through the Brazil-nut oil project," Petian says, "Paiakan is showing 23 his people another possibility for satisfying their economic needs. He's giving them a viable alternative[19] that includes helping to save the forest and their way of life."

"…Paiakan has a vision," Darrell Posey says. "He's trying in a lot of 24 ways to maintain his traditions—setting up a village school for Kayapo culture, creating a scientific reserve. At the same time he's making the transition to a modern world in which white men are not going to go away. He knows you either deal with them or you don't survive… ."

---

15 **timber rights**   ownership of the trees
16 **in vain**   for nothing
17 **unfolding**   happening
18 **afflicting**   harming
19 **viable alternative**   real choice

5. **On your own.** Look back at your questions in Activity 4 and write in any answers you found in the magazine article. After you finish, choose a question and answer to share with the class.

6. **On your own.** On another piece of paper, make a time line of Chief Paiakan's life. Even if you don't know dates for every event in his life, record the order of events.

READING STRATEGY:
Making a Time Line
See page 251.

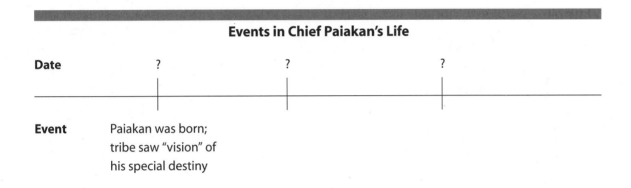

Events in Chief Paiakan's Life

| Date | ? | ? | ? |

Event Paiakan was born; tribe saw "vision" of his special destiny

After you finish the time line, get together with a partner. Without looking at your partner's time line, compare ideas.

7. **Group Work.** Have each person in your group choose a different topic from the list below. Look back over the reading to refresh your memory. Then, in your own words, tell the group what you know.

READING STRATEGY:
Paraphrasing
See page 253.

- Tell how Paiakan first tried to save his people.

- Tell what Paiakan did after he realized he and his people couldn't run forever.

- Tell what happened when Paiakan spoke out against the hydro-electric dam project.

- Tell what happened while Paiakan was away from the village on business.

▓▓▓▓▓▓▓▓▓▓▓▓▓▓▓

WRITING STRATEGY:
Using Quotations
See page 248.

8. Pair Work. Imagine what each person listed below might have said. Divide up the list and write possible quotations. (In parentheses are the paragraph numbers, if you need more information.)

Speaker/Context	Possible quotation
a. Paiakan, trying to convince his people of danger (5)	"The forest is our life. We must save the forest from people who will destroy it. If they destroy the forest, they destroy us," said Paiakan, pleading with his people.
b. a Kayapo villager, who does not believe Paiakan (6)	
c. Paiakan, telling his village of his decision to leave (8)	
d. Posey, an ethnobiologist, concerned for Paiakan's safety (11)	
e. an official of the government, reacting to criticism of the hydroelectric project (12)	
f. other Kayapo leaders, deciding to sell the village's timber rights during Paiakan's absence (18)	
g. Petian, an employee of The Body Shop (19, 23)	

After you finish, read your quotations to each other. Then double-check your punctuation (commas, quotation marks, periods). If you are unsure, look at how punctuation is used with direct quotations in the magazine article.

9. On your own. Use context to help you complete the sentences below. Your choices don't need to be the same as in the article, as long as they make sense in the context.

READING STRATEGY:
Using Context
See page 255.

a. Among the Kayapo, preparation for a new leader begins at birth. Such was the case for Paiakan, who is descended from a long line of chiefs. His father is a _____ peace-maker; and when Paiakan was born, the tribe received a "vision" of his special destiny.

b. "Our life is better here," Paiakan says [after moving farther away from the highway], "because this place is _____ in fish and game, with _____ soil."

c. But the new security did not last. During the 1980s, most other Kayapo villages in the Amazon were _____ affected by the relentless invasions. Along with _____ air and water came outbreaks of new diseases, requiring _____ medicines for treatment.

d. In June that year [1990], racing against time, Paiakan completed negotiations for Aukre to make its own money while _____ the forest. Working with The Body Shop, …he arranged for villagers to _____ Brazil nuts and then _____ a natural oil to be used in hair conditioners. It would be their first _____ to export.

After you finish, get together with a partner and share ideas. See if you agree on general meaning, even if you use different words to complete the sentences.

READING STRATEGY:
Making Inferences
See page 252.

10. **Pair Work.** The sentences below are from the magazine article on pages 116–119. Based on the information in these sentences, what inferences can you make? With your partner, draw some conclusions and write your thoughts on the lines.

a. "When I was still a boy," Paiakan recalls, "I knew that one day I would go into the world to learn what was coming to us." (Paragraph 2)

What do you infer about Paiakan?

_____

_____

_____

b. "…He [Paiakan] went to Belém, the state capital, where he learned to live, dress, and act like a white man. He learned to speak Portuguese, in order to communicate with government officials. He even taught himself to use a video camera, to document the destruction of the forest—so his people could see it for themselves and so the Kayapo children would know about it." (Paragraph 9)

What can you infer about Paiakan?

_____

_____

_____

c. "…[For speaking out against a project supported by the government,] Paiakan faced three years in prison and expulsion from the country; but when other Kayapo learned of his plight, some 400 leaders emerged from the forest in warpaint. The charges were dropped." (Paragraph 12)

124

What can you infer about the Kayapo?

What can you infer about the government?

_____

_____

_____

_____

_____

When you finish, get together with two other classmates and share ideas.

11. **On your own.** What does the quotation below mean to you? Write in your journal for five minutes without stopping. Some suggestions following the quotation may help you get started.

> "And I had to come out [of the forest,] to tell you that by destroying our environment, you're destroying your own." (Chief Paiakan)

> **CRITICAL THINKING STRATEGY:**
> *Interpreting*
> See page 262.

• How can "you" destroy your own environment by destroying Paiakan's?

• What do you think Paiakan's message is?

• How does the message relate to the title of this chapter, "Save a Village, Save the World?"

• What concrete example can you give to explain the message?

Share an idea from your journal writing with the class.

12. **Writing Project.** In writing, tell your classmates about someone who has worked to bring about social and/or political change. Choose someone other than Gandhi, Parks, or Paiakan, but the person doesn't need to be a well-known figure. The suggestions below may help you get started.

a. Spend time choosing someone you really want to write about. This might be someone whose name was added to the list in Activity 3.

b. After you decide, quickwrite about this person for five minutes, telling what the person has done to bring about change.

WRITING STRATEGY: *Quickwriting* See page 246.

Understanding Your Audience See page 247.

c. Since your classmates are your audience for this paper, consider what they might or might not know about this person. On separate paper, write down some questions you think you will need to answer.

   Example: *Did this person actually set out to change something or, like Rosa Parks, did it just happen?*

d. Tell a classmate about the person you are going to write about. Listen to your classmate's questions about this person. Make notes.

e. Look back at your quickwriting. Circle ideas you want to include in your paper. Look at the notes you took while listening to your classmate. Look at your questions above. Do you need more information before you start writing? Could you interview someone outside of class for more ideas? Can you find more information in the library?

WRITING STRATEGY: *Collecting Information* See page 238.

f. Focus your topic for a paper of roughly two pages. Decide on the most important points that you want to make.

g. From your notes, write a first draft of your paper.

h. Ask the classmate that you talked to earlier to read your draft. Does your classmate have other questions? If so, make notes in the margin of your draft for future work.

i. Place a copy of your draft in your writing folder.

CHAPTER FOUR

Can One Person Make a Difference?

1. **Class Work.** The essay on pages 129–131 is about a person whose work in her own neighborhood started a worldwide movement. Can you think of other individuals whose ideas or actions have brought about change? Brainstorm possibilities and write them on a cluster diagram on the board.

WRITING STRATEGY:
Making a Cluster Diagram
See page 241.

Brainstorming
See page 237.

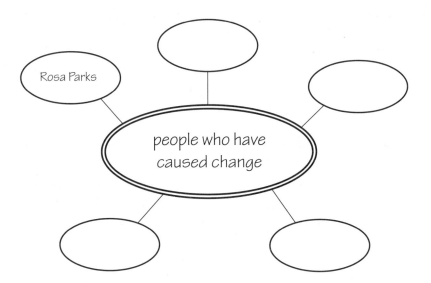

2. **On your own.** What can an individual do to bring about change? Choose one person from the cluster diagram as an example and write down some ideas.

   • What change did this person bring about?

   • How did this person cause change?

   • How do you explain the person's success?

   • What factors make change possible?

   Share an idea from your journal writing with your classmates.

WRITING STRATEGY:
Quickwriting
See page 246.

READING STRATEGY:
Previewing
See page 253.

3. Class Work. Read the title and the first four paragraphs on page 129 and answer the questions below.

a. What? _____

b. Who? _____

c. Where? _____

d. When? _____

With your classmates, predict what you will read about in the rest of the essay. Make a note of your prediction:

_____

_____

_____

_____

READING STRATEGY:
Finding Main Ideas
See page 250.

4. On your own. Read the essay from the beginning to check your prediction from Activity 3. As you read, also underline ideas that seem important to you.

Foresters Without Diplomas

By Wangari Maathai

from *Ms. Magazine*

We started with seven trees in 1977. By 1988, we had 10 million trees surviving.

1   The Green Belt movement started in my backyard. I was involved in a political campaign with a man I was married to; I was trying to see what I could do for the people who were helping us during our campaign, people who came from poor communities. I decided to create jobs for them— planting trees and shrubs, cleaning homes of the richer people in the communities, and getting paid for those services. That never worked, because poor people wanted support right away, and I didn't have money to pay them before the people we were working for had paid me. So I dropped the project but stayed with the idea. Then, in 1976—two years after the first backyard idea—I was invited to join the National Council of Women of Kenya.

2   We were into the U.N.'s "women's decade," and I got exposed to many of the problems women were facing—problems of firewood, malnutrition, lack of food and adequate water, unemployment, soil erosion.[1] Quite often what we see in the streets of our cities, in the rural areas, in the slums, are manifestations[2] of mistakes we make as we pretend we are "developing," as we pursue what we are now calling *maldevelopment.*

3   And so we decided to go to the women. Why? Well, I am a woman. I was in a women's organization. Women are the ones most affected by these problems. Women are concerned about children, about the future.

4   So we went to the women and talked about planting trees and overcoming, for example, such problems as the lack of firewood and building and fencing materials, stopping soil erosion, protecting water systems. The women agreed, although they didn't know how to do it.

5   The next few months we spent teaching them how to do it. We first called foresters to come and show the women how you plant trees. The foresters proved to be very complicated; because they have diplomas, they have complicated ways of dealing with a very simple thing like looking for

---

1 **soil erosion**   dirt washing or blowing away
2 **manifestations**   evidence, proof

seeds and planting trees. So eventually we taught the women to just do it using common sense. And they did. They were able to look for seeds in the neighborhood and learn to recognize seedlings[3] as they germinate when seeds fall on the ground. Women do not have to wait for anybody to grow trees. They are really foresters without diplomas.

We started on World Environment Day, June 5, 1977; that's when we 6 planted the first seven trees. Now, only two are still standing. They are beautiful nandi flame trees. The rest died. But by 1988, when we counted according to the records women sent back to us, we had 10 million trees surviving.[4] Many had already matured to be used by the women. But the most important thing is that the women were now independent; they had acquired knowledge, techniques; they had become empowered.[5] They have been teaching each other. We started with one tree nursery[6] in the backyard of the office of the National Council of Women. Today we have over 1,500 tree nurseries, 99 percent run by women... .

Funding is always a problem. We never received any financial support 7 from the Kenyan government. They gave us an office—which they took away as soon as we criticized them. (In a way, it is good they didn't give us

---

3 **seedlings**　young trees grown from seeds
4 **surviving**　living
5 **empowered**　strong, with power
6 **nursery**　a place for growing plants

One of the goals of the Green Belt movement is to stop soil erosion.

money because they would have withdrawn that.) We receive much of our support from abroad, mostly from women all over the world, who send us small checks. And the United Nations Development Fund for Women gave us a big boost, $100,000 in 1981. We also received support from the Danish Voluntary Fund and the Norwegian Agency for International Development. In the U.S., we are supported by the African Development Foundation, which helped us make a film about the Green Belt movement in 1985... .

8   In the field,[7] we now have about 750 people who teach new groups and help with the compilation of reports, which we monitor to have an idea of what is happening in the field. At the headquarters we now have about 40 people. When we were kicked out of our office, the headquarters[8] moved back to my house, a full circle return to where we started.

9   But it's 10 million trees later—not quite where we started. For myself, now that my two boys and a girl are big, when we have trained enough women in leadership and fund-raising, I would love to go back into an academic institution. I do miss it. My field is biology. But I was into micro-anatomy and developmental anatomy. I would love to be able to read more

---

7 **in the field**   working away from the central office
8 **headquarters**   the central office

about community development and motivation and write about the experience I have had in the field. And perhaps train people on grass-roots[9] projects. But that will have to wait. I earn maybe a tenth of what I could earn on the international market if I sold my expertise and energy, and I'm sure many people would probably consider me a fool. At home, the men don't believe that I don't make a fortune out of the Green Belt movement. But all over the world, we women do this sort of thing.

My greatest satisfaction is to look back and see how far we have come. [10] Something so simple but meaning so much, something nobody can take away from the people, something that is changing the face of the landscape.

But my greatest disappointment has been since I returned to Kenya in 1966 after my education in the United States. When I was growing up and going through school, I believed that the sky was the limit. I realized when I got home that the sky is not the limit, that human beings can make the limit for you, stop you from pursuing your full potential.[10] I have had to fight to make a contribution. We lose so much from people because we don't allow them to think freely and do when they can. So they lose their interest, their energy, the opportunity to be creative and positive. And developing countries need all the energy they can get.

I tell people that if they know how to read and write, it is an advan- [11] tage. But that all we really need is common sense and a desire to work. These are usually the last two things people are asked for. They are usually asked to use imposed knowledge[11] they do not relate to, so they become followers rather than leaders.

For example, because I criticized the political leadership, I have been [12] portrayed as a subversive, so it's very difficult for me not to feel constrained. I have the energy; I want to do exactly what they spend hours in the U.N. talking about. But when you really want to do it, you are not allowed, because the political system is not tolerant or encouraging enough.

But we must never lose hope. When any of us feels she has an idea or [13] an opportunity, she should go ahead and do it. I never knew when I was working in my backyard that what I was playing around with would one day become a whole movement. One person can make the difference.

---

9 **grass-roots**   local, at the level of *everyday* people
10 **your full potential**   all you are capable of doing
11 **imposed knowledge**   other people's knowledge, not yours

5. **Group Work.** See if you can define the words below. Go around the group, each person taking a turn. If one person can't define a word, go to the next person, and so on—until someone defines it. If nobody can, then circle the word and look it up.

a. community

b. firewood

c. malnutrition

d. unemployment

e. slums

f. soil erosion

g. common sense

h. motivation

i. expertise

j. fortune

k. neighborhood

l. knowledge

m. technique

n. fund-raising

o. satisfaction

p. potential

6. **Group Work.** Have each person in the group choose a topic from the list below. After looking back over the reading to refresh your memory, tell your group what you know—in your own words.

- Tell how the Green Belt movement got started.

- Tell why Maathai decided to work with women.

- Tell about the progress of the Green Belt movement.

- Tell how Maathai feels about her accomplishments.

> **READING STRATEGY:**
> *Paraphrasing*
> See page 253.

7. **Pair Work.** Read excerpts from Maathai's essay below and answer the questions that follow. Your answers will come from your understanding of the essay, which includes your own experience.

> **READING STRATEGY:**
> *Making Inferences*
> See page 252.

a. "Quite often what we see in the streets of our cities, in the rural areas, in the slums, are manifestations of mistakes we make as we pretend we are 'developing,' as we pursue what we are now calling *maldevelopment*."

What does Maathai think about past efforts to create social change?

_____

_____

_____

b. "I earn maybe a tenth of what I could earn on the international market if I sold my expertise and energy, and I'm sure many people would probably consider me a fool. At home, the men don't believe that I don't make a fortune out of the Green Belt movement. But all over the world, we women do this sort of thing."

Why does Maathai think that many people would consider her "a fool"? What assumption about women does Maathai make?

_____

_____

_____

c. "…[Common sense and a desire to work] are usually the last two things people are asked for. They are usually asked to use imposed knowledge they do not relate to, so they become followers rather than leaders."

How does Maathai think people become leaders?

_____

_____

_____

d. "When any of us feels she has an idea or opportunity, she should go ahead and do it. I never knew when I was working in my backyard that what I was playing around with would one day become a whole movement. One person can make the difference."

How would you characterize Maathai's outlook on life?

_____

_____

_____

When you finish, share your ideas with two other classmates.

8. **On your own.** What do you know about Wangari Maathai? Read through the essay again, collecting ideas to create a profile of her.

READING STRATEGY:
Reading for Specific Information
See page 254.

Profile of Wangari Maathai, founder of the Green Belt movement

wanted to help poor people

understood problems poor women were facing

_____

_____

_____

_____

_____

9. **On your own.** From the list above, choose an idea that interests you. Connect this idea to your own experience and write your ideas in your journal. Here are some questions you might think about as you write:

CRITICAL THINKING STRATEGY:
Synthesizing
See page 263.

- Who does this idea make you think of?

- How is this person like Maathai?

- Based on your own experience, do you agree or disagree with this idea? Why or why not?

10. **Writing Project.** *Can one person make a difference? Why or why not?* Write your ideas in an essay that might be published in a student magazine. Here are some suggestions to get you started.

WRITING STRATEGY:
Understanding Your Audience
See page 247.

   a. Think about which readers of the magazine need to hear your ideas. Students who take no interest in school? School administrators who don't give students opportunities to get involved? Who else? Decide who your readers are and what they need to know. Note your ideas below.

Who my readers are:

_____

What I want them to know:

_____

_____

b. Focus on the questions *Can one person make a difference? Why or why not?* What can you tell your readers to convince them of your ideas? What can you say to get them to believe you or do what you want them to do?

Make notes in your journal as you look through your quickwriting for ideas.

Narrow down your thinking to a focus that you can develop in two or three pages.

WRITING STRATEGY:
Focusing Your Ideas
See page 239.

Citing Sources
See page 237.

c. To your notes, add ideas and quotations from Maathai's essay on pages 129–131 and from the essays about Ghandi on pages 94–96, Parks on pages 105–108, or Paiakan on pages 116–119. Be sure to cite your sources.

Example: *Rosa Parks had not planned to start a civil rights movement the day she refused to give up her seat on the bus. She had just had enough, she said later, and wanted to be treated like a human being.* (Marie Ragghianti, *Parade Magazine*)

d. Drawing from your notes, write a first draft.

e. Ask a classmate to read your draft. Does your classmate have questions? Make notes in the margin about ideas you might change or add at a later time.

f. Place your draft in your writing folder.

g. You might check to see if there actually is a school magazine that might publish your paper at a later time. If not, you and your classmates might consider starting a class magazine or school magazine.

UNIT THREE
Final Project

You now have four pieces of writing from Unit Three, one from the writing assignment at the end of each chapter. Each is a rough draft—a collection of first ideas.

Choose one of these drafts to revise. It doesn't matter which one you choose, but you will probably want to choose the one you like best. Before you start revising, though, read through the notes below.

Notes on Revising

From your earlier final projects, you already know three reasons to revise:

- to sharpen your focus
- to make your writing interesting to your readers
- to help your readers follow your ideas

Before you start revising your first draft, think about how you can help your readers follow your ideas.

☑ *Revising to help readers follow your ideas*

1. **Use your title to direct your readers.** The title serves as a reader's "road sign." From your title, readers know the direction of your thinking.

   Example: *writing about Rosa Parks' role in the U.S. Civil Rights movement*

Unhelpful titles	Helpful titles
Civil Rights	*Having the Courage to Say No*
Freedom	*One Brave Act Launches a Movement*

2. **Use your introduction to guide your readers.** By the end of the introduction, readers need to understand what the writer is "promising" to do.

Example: *writing about someone who helps bring about social change*

Unhelpful introduction	**Helpful introduction**
Martin Luther King received world recognition for his work when he received the Nobel Peace Prize. Brother Joseph Webre, unknown outside his own community, founded a program to feed the hungry of New Orleans. Mohandas Gandhi is revered by Indians as the founder of their nation. Rosa Park's act of courage started the U.S. Civil Rights movement.	*By 7:00 every morning, Brother Joseph Webre leaves the bakery of St. Joseph Abbey to deliver the 700 loaves of bread that he and other monks have baked. Father Joe is the founder of Pennies for Bread, a program that gives both food and hope to the poor of New Orleans. Unknown, except by the hundreds who receive his gift of love, Father Joe is one of many people working quietly to bring about social change in their own communities.*

3. **Organize your ideas clearly.** Readers expect you to keep the promise you make when you introduce your topic. They also expect some familiar plan of organization, as they follow your thinking. Some plans familiar to readers of English are these:

   a. **evidence leading to a conclusion, or a conclusion supported by evidence**

   Example:

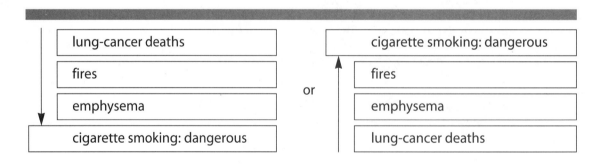

b. **cause and effect (analyzing "why" and/or "so what")**

Example:

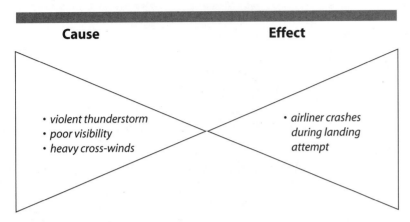

Cause   **Effect**

- *violent thunderstorm*
- *poor visibility*
- *heavy cross-winds*

- *airliner crashes during landing attempt*

c. **process (analyzing "how" or "how to")**

Example:

How volcanos erupt

STEP 1: hot molten rock mixes with gas to form magma
STEP 2: magma collects in chambers
STEP 3: surrounding rock exerts pressure
STEP 4: magma begins to rise

d. **comparison (analyzing sameness or difference)**

Example:

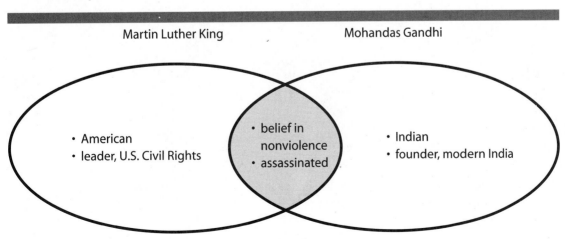

Martin Luther King   Mohandas Gandhi

- American
- leader, U.S. Civil Rights

- belief in nonviolence
- assassinated

- Indian
- founder, modern India

e. **narrative (telling a story to make a point)**

Example:

NEED TO BAN HANDGUNS

...child finds father's gun

  ...child plays with gun

    ...child accidentally shoots friend

f. **definition (analyzing, often in order to evaluate)**

Example: *nonviolent resistance*

• strategy for achieving political and social change

• way to practice civil disobedience

• highlights violence of opposition

• used effectively by Martin Luther King and Mohandas Gandhi

When you first put your ideas down on paper, you aren't thinking about a particular plan. When you revise, though, you need to put yourself in your reader's shoes. Your reader will be more comfortable following a familiar path. Which plan is better? That all depends on you, your topic, your purpose in writing, and your audience.

We asked Amanda Buege, an experienced writer, for ideas on making writing clear.

Making Your Writing Clear

Because I'm a writing instructor as well as a graduate student, I am in the unique position to teach *and* learn at the same time. What I learn about writing in my classes, I try to pass on to my students. Above all, I stress to my students that their writing has to be clear. Making my own writing clear is something I work hard at, especially when I'm revising.

But clear writing isn't always so easy to teach or learn. Sometimes shorter, more succinct[1] sentences make ideas clearer. Other times, clarity[2] comes by way of adding sentences. As I reread, I say to myself, "Can I find sentences that need stronger images, more details, or better examples? Can I say the same thing in more precise language?"

Recently, a student questioned me after I wrote "unclear" in the margin of her essay. In her essay about homelessness in America, she had written, "Oftentimes people look at them and don't even see homeless people." She was commenting on the "invisibility factor" of the homeless—how we people with homes no longer notice homeless people on our city streets, any more than we notice litter[3] on the sidewalk or graffitti[4] on the walls of abandoned buildings.

I tried to tell my student that her point was a good one, but that she needed to reword the troublesome sentence to make her meaning clear. I pointed out that she had used the word "people" twice in one short sentence, with two different groups in mind, and that the meaning of "them," while obviously referring to the homeless, was not really clear. I wanted my student to consider more precise wording or to use an image, such as litter or graffitti, for readers to better understand her idea.

Overall, here is what I tell my students about revising for clarity. When I reread the first time for clarity, I start at the very top—with the title. I always keep in mind that a title should be interesting and informative. A good title is my reader's first "road sign"; it should tell my reader where my writing is "headed."

After the title, I move to my thesis.[5] Is it clear, precise, and appropriate for the length of my paper? If the assignment is to write a 400-500 word essay on hunger, then I know not to tackle[6] the issue of world hunger in so few words. While revising, I make sure the focus of my essay is limited. Is my topic, the need for

---

1 **succinct**   concise, saying a lot in a few words
2 **clarity**   being clear
3 **litter**   trash
4 **graffitti**   writing or drawings on walls
5 **thesis**   a writer's most comprehensive idea, or claim
6 **tackle**   try to do something difficult

neighborhood food banks in New Orleans—for example, the right size for the assignment? Not only is the size right, but is my thesis clear?

As I continue to reread my writing, I check for organization (overall clarity) and sentence clarity. I add words, subtract words, and rewrite whole paragraphs. I may repeat the process five, even six times! It isn't easy for me to make my writing clear. But I always try to remember that what I have to say is important. The clearer my writing, the better my chance at communicating with my reader. And isn't communicating what writing is all about?

—Amanda Buege

Process of Revising

As you start revising your first draft, here are some suggestions:

❖ **Writing a second draft.** Use the revising checklist on page 143 to evaluate your first draft. From your evaluation, decide what changes you want to make and note them in the margin of your paper. When you are ready, work from your notes and write a new draft.

❖ **Writing a third draft.** Ask a classmate to read your second draft and complete the revising checklist. From your classmate's evaluation and your own ideas, decide what changes you want to make. Note the changes in the margin of your paper. When you are ready, work from your notes and write a new draft.

❖ **Writing additional drafts.** Repeat any part of the process until you are satisfied with your writing. Your teacher may want to use the checklist to evaluate your final draft.

Unit Three
Revising Checklist

Yes ✓

	First draft	Second draft	Third draft	Final draft
Sharpening your focus				
• Is it clear who the audience is?	❑	❑	❑	❑
• Is the topic limited enough?	❑	❑	❑	❑
• Have unnecessary words been deleted?	❑	❑	❑	❑
Making your writing interesting				
• Does the introduction "hook" the reader?	❑	❑	❑	❑
• Does the writer use interesting details?	❑	❑	❑	❑
• Does the writer's voice come through?	❑	❑	❑	❑
Helping your reader follow your ideas				
• Does the title suggest the writer's thinking?	❑	❑	❑	❑
• Does the introduction guide the reader?	❑	❑	❑	❑
• Can the reader perceive the writer's plan?	❑	❑	❑	❑

UNIT FOUR
Language in Conflict

In this unit you will read four selections related to the theme of conflict.

- From looking at these photographs, what conflicts can you imagine?
- How do you think language can be a source of conflict?

CHAPTER ONE

Losing Your Language

WRITING STRATEGY:
Brainstorming
See page 237.

1. **Group Work.** Brainstorm answers to the question below. Have one member of the group record your answers.

   How can a language be lost? (Under what circumstances?)

   Example: *Some people move to a foreign country and live where no one speaks their language. Gradually, they start speaking only the language of the surrounding community.*

   Choose someone in the group to report your group's ideas to the class. Ask your teacher or a classmate to write the ideas on the board.

WRITING STRATEGY:
Quickwriting
See page 246.

2. **On your own.** Choose an idea from Activity 1 and quickwrite in your journal. Write for five minutes without stopping. Below are some questions that might help you get started.

   • Do you know anyone who has lost his/her language in this way? What were the effects on the person? The effects on the family?

   • Are you afraid you might lose your language in this way? Why or why not?

   Choose an idea from your journal writing to share with the class.

CRITICAL THINKING STRATEGY:
Applying What You Know
See page 259.

3. **Class Work.** Based on the following details, what general claims can you make? Share ideas with your classmates.

   a. According to the *Oxford English Dictionary,* the last known speaker of Cornish, the Celtic language of Cornwall in south-western England, died in the late 1700s.

      How can a language be lost?

      _____

b. According to a recent article in the *Washington Post,* Native American children in Oklahoma (USA) were punished at school for speaking their home language.

How can a language be lost?

_____

c. A recent article in the *San Francisco Examiner* tells about a young man who became so "American" that he could not communicate with his parents in their native Spanish.

How can a language be lost?

_____

d. In *Hunger of Memory,* Richard Rodriguez writes about the day his teachers came to his house and told his parents not to speak Spanish at home so that he would learn English faster.

How can a language be lost?

_____

4. **Class Work.** Look over your claims from Activity 3 and compare different ways languages can be lost. Below are some questions you might ask.

- In the first situation *(a),* what are the implications for the Cornish language?

- Might the implications be the same for Native American languages *(b)?*

- How do you think *a* and *c* are different?

- To you, are *c* and *d* different? Why or why not?

- In *c* and *d,* what effects on the family can you imagine?

CRITICAL THINKING
STRATEGY:
Analyzing
See page 258.

ⵣⵏⵍⵉⵏⵡⵏⵉⵍⵏⵡⵏⵍⵉⵏⵡⵏⵉⵏⵡ

READING STRATEGY:
Previewing
See page 253.

5. Pair Work. The passage below is from the newspaper article on pages 149–150. After you read the passage, turn to the article and look at the title and photographs. Tell your partner what you think the article is about.

> "So many of the elders were punished for using their native language," she said. "The authorities thought they would always know what the students were talking about if they didn't use their language. They were also trying to pull the young Indians out of their culture."

ⵣⵏⵍⵉⵏⵡⵏⵉⵍⵏⵡⵏⵍⵉⵏⵡⵏⵉⵏⵡ

READING STRATEGY:
Writing Margin Notes
See page 257.

6. On your own. Read the newspaper article on pages 149–150. As you read, make notes in the margin about ideas you find important and interesting.

Oklahoma Students Start the Day With an *O-si-yo* for Teacher

by Sue Anne Pressley

from *The Boston Globe*

1 **Oaks, Oklahoma**—In Lucinda Turtle's class, second graders are learning colors and numbers and everyday phrases.

> *Hello: O-si-yo.*
> *Green: I-je-yu-sdi*
> *Seven: Galigwogi*

2 This is Cherokee, a language that some of the children still hear at home from their grandmothers or elderly[1] uncles. Sometimes, Nathan Soap's mother uses the brisk, barking[2] tones when she speaks to his grandmother, and he wonders what secrets the women are sharing.

3 "They might be talking about me," the alert 7 year-old said.

4 Discouraged for decades by authorities intent on assimilation,[3] more than a dozen old Native American languages are making a comeback[4] this year in Oklahoma public schools.

5 A new state law that took effect with the 1993–94 academic term ordered the schools to provide second-language studies to students of all ages, an opportunity seized[5] by officials of the state's Indian Education Office to revive the dying languages and cultures of Oklahoma's 36 tribes.

6 Thus, instead of Spanish and French, for instance, some students are learning Cherokee, Creek, Choctaw, Chickasaw or Seminole.

7 For Valeria Littlecreek, the state's director of Indian education, the program has a special poignance.[6] She remembers her mother, Christine Henneha, now 63, telling tales about being struck with a ruler as a child or

---

1 **elderly** old
2 **brisk, barking** fast, sharp
3 **assimilation** making the minority culture part of the majority culture
4 **comeback** return
5 **seized** acted on
6 **poignance** emotional meaning

having her mouth washed out with soap if she slipped[7] and spoke her Creek language. As a result, Littlecreek, 38, learned only a few Creek words from her mother.

"So many of the elders were punished for using their native language," [8] she said. "The authorities thought they would always know what the students were talking about if they didn't use their language. They were also trying to pull the young Indians out of their culture.

"Now we know that you can't separate your language from your culture, and it's all going to die out unless we keep it up. Maybe we're not going to produce that many fluent speakers, but we had to start somewhere." [9]

Northeastern Oklahoma is headquarters for the Cherokee Nation,[8] and [10] many of the schools in this hilly farming country, including the Oaks-Mission School where Turtle teaches, are focusing on the Cherokee language, whose alphabet was devised in 1821.

While 727,000 Native American children attend Oklahoma public [11] schools, the native languages program, launched in 14 school districts so far, is not limited solely to them. At Oaks-Mission, 85 percent Cherokee, all 425 students in preschool classes through high school are learning how to say *i-ya (pumpkin)* and *selu (corn).*

Kindergartners play fishing games, hooking paper fish with numbers [12]

---

7 **slipped** made a mistake
8 **Nation** tribe

150

and colors written on them. Fourth graders play Cherokee Bingo, the blocks on their cards filled with words such as *da la du (sixteen)* and *da-lo-ni-ge (yellow)*. Twelfth graders write the difficult, curving characters of the alphabet, creating sample menus featuring *a-wi-ha-wi-ya (deer meat)*.

13   The spellings Turtle uses in her classroom, she said, are simply English sounds enabling the children to pronounce the Cherokee words.

14   "The Indian children, they've lost the language," said Turtle, 43, a former fourth-grade teacher whose first language is Cherokee. "Pretty much anymore, the only ones who speak it are the grandparents."

15   Turtle said she feels a great deal of pride in helping to restore the Cherokee language and culture. She intersperses[9] flash-card performances with the recounting of Old Cherokee tales, such as the one about the Fox and the crawdad. The moral of this story is: Don't tell lies.

16   "The dying out of the language was partially our fault," Turtle said. "I speak Cherokee, but I didn't teach it to my two kids. Now I use it more around the house. Everybody's favorite is *o-sta di, time to eat.*

---

9 **intersperses**   puts in from time to time

7. On your own. Drawing from your margin notes and the ideas below, write a summary of the newspaper article. Write just enough to "jog" your memory about the article, if you were to read your summary a month from now.

Possible notes on *o-si-yo* article:

> *authorities intent on assimilation*
>
> *elders punished for using their native language*
>
> *state law ordered schools to provide second-language studies*
>
> *Native American languages making comeback*
>
> *revive dying languages and cultures of Oklahoma's 36 tribes*

Get together with a partner and read each other's summaries. Compare the two. What is different? What is the same?

8. Pair Work. Share ideas with a partner in answering the questions below. Your answers will come from your understanding of the article, which includes your own experience.

a. Why does Nathan Soap think his mother and grandmother are sharing secrets?

_____

b. Why do you think the Oklahoma authorities were against Native American languages?

_____

c. Why does the native languages program have a special poignance for Valeria Littlecreek?

_____

d. Why did Littlecreek learn very little Creek from her mother?

_____

e. Why do you think *all* school children are included in the new native languages program?

_____

f. Why are menus, stories, and words for food included in the language lessons described in the newspaper article?

_____

g. What do some of the family names included in the article *(Turtle, Soap, Littlecreek)* tell you about Native American cultures?

_____

Get together with two other classmates to compare ideas. If you disagree on some ideas, explain your thinking to each other.

9. **On your own.** Choose an idea from the *o-si-yo* article that interests you. Connect this idea to your own experience and write your ideas in your journal. Below are some questions you might think about as you write.

   • What does this idea remind you of?

   • Based on your own experience and knowledge, do you agree or disagree with this idea? Why?

   • How do you think you would react under the same circumstances?

   Tell a classmate about an idea from your journal writing.

CRITICAL THINKING STRATEGY: *Synthesizing* See page 263.

10. **Writing Project.** *Does it matter if people lose their language? Why or why not?* Write your ideas in a letter to authorities intent on assimilation. Here are some suggestions to get you started:

   a. Decide on which authorities need to hear your ideas: School authorities who punish students for speaking their home language at school? Government officials who don't support language programs? Someone else? Note your ideas below.

WRITING STRATEGY: *Understanding Your Audience* See page 247.

Who my audience is:

_____

What I want to persuade them to do:

_____

_____

▣◈▥◈▥◈▥◈▥◈▣

WRITING STRATEGY:
Citing Sources
See page 237.

b. Focus on the questions *Does it matter if people lose their language? Why or why not?* Review your journal writing and circle ideas you might use. Make notes.

To your notes, add ideas from the *o-si-yo* article on pages 149–150. Your margin notes should help you find ideas. Be sure to cite your source.

Example: *According to Valeria Littlecreek, the Oklahoma Director of Indian Education, "…we know that you can't separate your language from your culture…." (Washington Post)*

c. Check other material for ideas and useful quotations. You might look for ideas that show how important language is to people.

Either of the following quotations might be useful to you:

"I write in English. But everything I write about comes from my experience as a Spanish-speaker. My English is much richer because I grew up in a Spanish-speaking family. I feel lucky because I have twice as many words to choose from as other writers."

> —Sandra Cisneros, a Mexican-American poet and writer, in an interview published in US Express

"My parents would say something to me and I would feel embraced by the sounds of their words. Those sounds said: I am speaking with ease in Spanish. I am addressing you in words I never use with los gringos. I recognize you as someone special, like no one outside. You belong with us. In the family."

> —Richard Rodriguez, a Mexican-American writer, in an essay entitled "Aria"

d. Decide which important points you want to argue. To help you decide, quickwrite in your journal for 5–10 minutes in response to the questions below:

WRITING STRATEGY:
Focusing Your Ideas
See page 239.

- What do you want these authorities to do? Change their thinking? Change their attitude? Cause something to happen?

- What ideas will convince them to do it?

- What details can you use to explain and support your ideas?

- Whose words can you cite to make your argument stronger?

e. Drawing from your notes and your quickwriting, write a first draft of a paper.

f. Ask a friend outside of class to read your draft and ask you questions.

g. From your friend's questions, make notes to yourself in the margin about ideas you might change or add at a later time.

h. Place the draft, with your notes, in your writing folder.

Problems with Language

1. **Class Work.** The essay on pages 158–160 is about a young man who has trouble reading. Why might a person have trouble reading? Brainstorm some possible reasons and write them on a cluster diagram on the board.

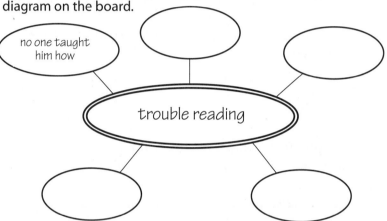

2. **Pair Work.** With a partner, read the title of the newspaper article on page 158 and the italicized information following the title. Tell each other what you expect to read about. The definition below might help.

> *Dyslexia (dis-lék-se-ə) is a term used for certain difficulties in learning to read. Dyslexic children are thought to have problems in separating language into distinct sounds at a critical time when this skill is required for learning to read. If a child does not perceive that the spoken language can be split into separate units (sounds, words, sentences), then the child will not perceive the connection between the spoken units and symbols that can be written and read. (from Children with Speech and Language Difficulties by Webster & McConnell. London: Cassell Educational Ltd., 1987)*

Then take turns reading the first sentence of each paragraph to each other and tell each other what you know about David Raymond.

3. Pair Work. What problems might a person with dyslexia have at school and at home? List your ideas in the left column of the chart below.

Effects of dyslexia

Our ideas	David Raymond's experience
other kids make fun of you	

4. On your own. *What did David Raymond experience as a result of dyslexia?* Keep this question in mind as you read the article on pages 158–160. Underline information and ideas that will help you answer the question.

When you finish reading, work from your underlining and fill in the right column of the chart in Activity 3. Compare the two columns and report differences to the class.

> READING STRATEGY:
> *Reading for*
> *Specific Information*
> See page 254.

On Being 17, Bright,[1] and Unable to Read

by David Raymond

from *The New York Times*

When the following article appeared in The New York Times, *David Raymond was a high school student in Connecticut. In his essay, he poignantly discusses his great difficulty in reading because of dyslexia and the many problems he experienced in school as a result.*

One day a substitute teacher picked me to read aloud from the textbook. When I told her, "No, thank you," she came unhinged. She thought I was acting smart, and told me so. I kept calm, and that got her madder and madder. We must have spent 10 minutes trying to solve the problem, and finally she got so red in the face I thought she'd blow up. She told me she'd see me after class. 1

Maybe someone like me was a new thing for that teacher. But she wasn't new to me. I've been through scenes like that all my life. You see, even though I'm 17 and a junior in high school, I can't read because I have dyslexia. I'm told I read "at a fourth-grade level," but from where I sit, that's not reading. You can't know what that means unless you've been there. It's not easy to tell how it feels when you can't read your homework assignments or the newspaper or a menu in a restaurant or even notes from your own friends. 2

My family began to suspect[2] I was having problems almost from the first day I started school. My father says my early years in school were the worst years of his life. They weren't so good for me, either. As I look back on it now, I can't find the words to express how bad it really was. I wanted to die. I'd come home from school screaming, "I'm dumb.[3] I'm dumb—I wish I were dead!" 3

I guess I couldn't read anything at all then—not even my own name— and they tell me I didn't talk as good as other kids. But what I remember 4

---

1 **bright**   intelligent
2 **suspect**   become aware
3 **dumb**   stupid

158

about those days is that I couldn't throw a ball where it was supposed to go, I couldn't learn to swim, and I wouldn't learn to ride a bike, because no matter what anyone told me, I knew I'd fail.

5   Sometimes my teachers would try to be encouraging. When I couldn't read the words on the board, they'd say, "Come on, David, you know that word." Only I didn't. And it was embarrassing. I just felt dumb. And dumb was how the kids treated me. They'd make fun of me every chance they got, asking me to spell "cat" or something like that. Even if I knew how to spell it, I wouldn't; they'd only give me another word. Anyway, it was awful, because more than anything I wanted friends. On my birthday when I blew out the candles I didn't wish I could learn to read; what I wished for was that the kids would like me.

6   With the bad reports coming from school, and with me moaning about wanting to die and how everybody hated me, my parents began looking for help. That's when the testing started. The school tested me, the child-guidance center tested me, private psychiatrists tested me. Everybody knew something was wrong—especially me.

7   It didn't help much when they stuck a fancy name on it.[4] I couldn't pronounce it then—I was only in second grade—and I was ashamed to talk about it. Now it rolls off my tongue, because I've been living with it for a lot of years—*dyslexia*.

8   All through elementary school it wasn't easy. I was always having to do things that were "different," things the other kids didn't have to do. I had to go to a child psychiatrist, for instance.

9   One summer my family forced me to go to a camp[5] for children with reading problems. I hated the idea, but the camp turned out pretty good, and I had a good time. I met a lot of kids who couldn't read and somehow that helped. The director of the camp said I had a higher I.Q.[6] than 90 percent of the population. I didn't believe him.

10   About the worst thing I had to do in fifth and sixth grade was go to a special education class in another school in our town. A bus picked me up, and I didn't like that at all. The bus also picked up emotionally disturbed[7] kids and retarded[8] kids. It was like going to a school for the retarded. I always worried that someone I know would see me on that bus. It was a relief to go to the regular junior high school.

---

4 **stuck a fancy name on it**   gave it a technical name
5 **camp**   place with cabins and outdoor space, with fun activities
6 **I.Q.**   intelligence
7 **emotionally disturbed**   with emotional problems
8 **retarded**   with low intelligence

Life began to change a little for me then, because I began to feel better 11 about myself. I found the teachers cared; they had meetings about me and I worked harder for them for a while. I began to work on the potter's wheel, making vases and pots that the teachers said were pretty good. Also, I got a letter[9] for being on the track team. I could always run pretty fast.

At high school, the teachers are good and everyone is trying to help me. 12 I've gotten honors some marking periods and I've won a letter on the cross-country team. Next quarter I think the school might hold a show of my pottery. I've got some friends. But there are still some embarrassing times. For instance, every time there is writing in the class, I get up and go to the special education room. Kids ask me where I go all the time. Sometimes I say "to Mars."

Homework is a real problem. During free periods in school I go into the 13 special ed room and staff members read assignments to me. When I get home my mother reads to me. Sometimes she reads an assignment into a tape recorder, and then I go into my room and listen to it. If we have a novel or something like that to read, she reads it out loud to me. Then I sit down with her and we do the assignment. She'll write, while I talk my answers to her. Lately, I've taken to dictating into a tape recorder, and then someone— my father, a private tutor, or my mother—types up what I've dictated. Whatever homework I do takes someone else's time too. That makes me feel bad.

We had a big meeting in school the other day—eight of us, four from 14 the guidance department, my private tutor, my parents, and me. The subject was me. I said I wanted to go to college, and they told me about colleges that have facilities and staff to handle people like me. That's nice to hear.

As for what happens after college, I don't know and I'm worried about 15 that. How can I make a living if I can't read? Who will hire me? How will I fill out the application form? The only thing that gives me any courage is the fact that I've learned about well-known people who couldn't read or had other problems and still made it. Like Albert Einstein, who didn't talk until he was 4 and flunked math. Like Leonardo da Vinci, who everyone seems to think had dyslexia.

I've told this story because some teacher will read it and go easy on a kid 16 in the classroom who has what I've got. Or, maybe some parent will stop nagging his kid, and stop calling him lazy. Maybe he's not lazy or dumb. Maybe he just can't read and doesn't know what's wrong. Maybe he's scared, like I was.

---

9 **letter** an award to athletes

5. On your own. Read the lines below from David Raymond's story. Imagine you are David's father and quickwrite for 5–10 minutes in your journal, telling about David's early years from "your" point of view as his father.

┌─────────────────────────┐
│ **WRITING STRATEGY:** │
│ *Using Point of View* │
│ See page 247. │
└─────────────────────────┘

> "My father says my early years in school were the worst years of his life." (Paragraph 3)

Tell a classmate about an idea from your journal writing.

6. Pair Work. Use context—the words and ideas around an unfamiliar word—to guess the meaning of the underlined words in the sentences below. Then share ideas with two other classmates.

┌─────────────────────────┐
│ **READING STRATEGY:** │
│ *Using Context* │
│ See page 255. │
└─────────────────────────┘

a. "When I told her, 'No, thank you,' she <u>came unhinged</u>. She thought I was acting smart, and told me so. I kept calm, and that got her madder and madder." (Paragraph 1)

Our guess: _____

b. "We must have spent 10 minutes trying to solve the problem, and finally she got so red in the face I thought she'd <u>blow up</u>." (Paragraph 1)

Our guess: _____

c. "Sometimes my teachers would try to be <u>encouraging</u>. When I couldn't read the words on the board they'd say, 'Come on, David, you know that word.'" (Paragraph 5)

Our guess: _____

d. "It didn't help much when they stuck a fancy name on it. I couldn't pronounce it then—I was only in second grade—and I was <u>ashamed</u> to talk about it." (Paragraph 7)

Our guess: _____

READING STRATEGY:
Making Inferences
See page 252.

7. Pair Work. What can you figure out about David Raymond's feeling and his state of mind from the details below? Write your ideas on the lines.

a. "It's not easy to tell how it feels when you can't read your home-work assignments or the newspaper or a menu in a restaurant or even notes from your own friends." (Paragraph 2)

How do you think David felt?

_____

b. "I wanted to die. I'd come home from school screaming, 'I'm dumb. I'm dumb—I wish I were dead!'" (Paragraph 3)

What would you say about David's state of mind?

_____

c. "But what I remember about those days is that I couldn't throw a ball where it was supposed to go, I couldn't learn to swim, and I wouldn't learn to ride a bike, because no matter what anyone told me, I knew I'd fail." (Paragraph 4)

What can you tell about David's level of confidence?

_____

d. "On my birthday when I blew out the candles I didn't wish I could learn to read; what I wished for was that the kids would like me." (Paragraph 5)

What can you say about David's needs?

_____

e. "The bus also picked up emotionally disturbed kids and retarded kids. It was like going to a school for the retarded. I always worried that someone I knew would see me on that bus." (Paragraph 10)

What does this tell you about David's concerns?

_____

When you finish, share your ideas with the class.

8. **Group Work.** Look at David Raymond's story with a writer's eye. You probably noticed that David's writing sounds a lot like speaking. (*Diction* is the word for a writer's tone and rhythm.) Find at least ten examples of words and phrases in David's writing that make his diction *conversational*.

CRITICAL THINKING STRATEGY: *Analyzing* See page 258.

Examples of conversational diction

she came unhinged   I thought she'd blow up (paragraph 1)

_____

_____

_____

_____

_____

Why do you think David writes this way? Support your ideas with lines from the text that help explain your analysis. When you finish, have one member of the group report your group's ideas to the class.

9. **On your own.** Choose three questions below to answer in writing.

CRITICAL THINKING STRATEGY: *Evaluating* See page 261.

   a. **Paragraph 1:** What is your opinion of the way the teacher responded to David?

   _____

   _____

   b. **Paragraph 6:** Do you think David's parents did the right thing? Why or why not?

   _____

   _____

c. **Paragraph 9:** Was it good for David to go to a camp for children with reading problems? Why or why not?

_____

_____

d. **Paragraphs 14–15:** What do you think about David's future plans and his concerns? What advice can you give him?

_____

_____

When you finish, share your ideas with a partner.

| WRITING STRATEGY: |
| *Listing Ideas* |
| See page 241. |

10. **Pair Work.** What aspects of David Raymond's childhood were the most difficult, in your opinion? List them below to the left. Then look back at the earlier reading on pages 158–160. What difficulties might Valerie Littlecreek's mother, Christine Henneha, have had as a child? List those ideas to the right.

David Raymond's difficulties	Christine Henneha's difficulties

Do the two lists have anything in common? When you finish, share ideas with the class.

11. **Writing Project.** What do you find interesting about David Raymond's experience? What about David's experience relates to other people's experiences? In the ideas that come to mind, look for a topic to write about. In academic classes, your teachers will often expect you to choose your own topic and connect it to the subject of the course.

These suggestions might help you get started:

a. How can you connect David's experience to the experience of other children with special language needs? Look through your journal writing for ideas to write about. List them below.

Possible topics for this writing assignment:

_____

_____

WRITING STRATEGY:
Finding a Topic
See page 239.

b. Choose an idea you like and write about it for 5–10 minutes in your journal. Do you think this idea will work as the focus of your paper? If you can't "get anywhere" with it, choose another one and quickwrite again.

c. Decide who your audience is: Parents? Teachers? Child guidance counselors? Someone else? Make a note below.

Audience: _____

List questions your audience might want you to answer:

_____

_____

WRITING STRATEGY:
Quickwriting
See page 246.

Understanding Your Audience
See page 247.

d. From readings in this unit, make notes in your journal of ideas and quotations to use in your paper.

e. Drawing from your notes, write a first draft of your paper.

f. Ask a friend outside of class to read the draft and ask you questions. From your friend's questions, make notes in the margin of the draft for future work.

g. Place the draft in your writing folder.

WRITING STRATEGY:
Providing Details
See page 246.

CHAPTER THREE

Two Languages, Two Worlds

1. **Group Work.** Read the title of the poem on page 167 and the possible "conversation" below. What do you think the poem is about? Does the conversation make sense to you? Why or why not? Share ideas with each other.

   Question: What do you say in Athabaskan* when you leave each other? What is the word for *good-bye?*

   Answer: We just say *Tlaa.* That means *see you.* We never leave each other. When does your mouth say good-bye to your heart?

2. **Group Work.** Based on the conversation above and your own experience, what do you think is difficult about translating from one language to another? Write your ideas below.

   Difficulty of translating from one language to another:

   _____

   _____

   _____

   _____

   Choose someone in the group to report your group's ideas to the class.

3. **Class Work.** Listen as your teacher reads the poem on page 167–168 aloud several times. Then read it aloud with a partner.

---

* Athabaskan is a Native American language.

There Is No Word for Goodbye

by Mary TallMountain

Sokoya,[1] I said, looking through
       the net of wrinkles[2] into
       wise black pools
       of her eyes.

What do you say in Athabaskan
       when you leave each other?
       What is the word
       for goodbye?

A shade of feeling rippled[3]
       the wind-tanned skin
       Ah, nothing, she said,
       watching the river flash.[4]

She looked at me close.
       We just say, Tlaa. That means,
       See you.
       We never leave each other.
       When does your mouth
       say goodbye to your heart?

---

1 **Sokoya**   maternal aunt
2 **wrinkles**   lines in the skin showing age
3 **rippled**   moved like little waves on water
4 **flash**   shine

She touched me light
      as a bluebell.[5]
      You forget when you leave us,
      You're so small then.
      We don't use that word.

We always think you're coming back,
      but if you don't,
      we'll see you some place else.
      You understand.
      There is no word for goodbye.

---

4 **bluebell**   a little blue flower with petals shaped like bells

ABOUT THE AUTHOR

A native of Alaska, Mary TallMountain is part Russian, Scots-Irish, and Athabaskan. She is the author of *Nine Poems* (1979) and *There Is No Word for Goodbye* (1981), of which this is the title poem.

4. **Class Work.** Do you like the TallMountain poem? Why or why not? The questions below might help start your discussion.

   • What do you like about the poem?

   • In your opinion, which lines are the most "powerful"?

   • Which words create strong images (pictures) in your mind?

   • Do you think Sokoya's words are important? Why or why not?

CRITICAL THINKING STRATEGY: *Evaluating* See page 261.

5. **On your own.** Quickwrite for five minutes in your journal about the poem. The questions below might help you get started.

   • If there is no word for *good-bye* in Athabaskan, what does this tell you about Athabaskan culture?

   • If you learned to speak Athabaskan, how might you change your way of thinking?

   • Look at the title of this chapter of the textbook. What connection can you make between the title—*Two Languages, Two Worlds*—and the poem?

   You might pick one of your ideas to share with the class.

CRITICAL THINKING STRATEGY: *Interpreting* See page 262.

6. **On your own.** Read the title of the essay on page 167 and the italicized information that follows it. From that information, what do you think the phrase, *the misery of silence,* means? Share ideas with your classmates.

7. **On your own.** Read the essay on pages 167–168 and underline ideas that seem important to you. When you finish, return to Activity 6 and see if you agree with your prediction.

READING STRATEGY: *Predicting* See page 253.

Finding Main Ideas See page 250.

The Misery of Silence

by Maxine Hong Kingston

Growing up in California as the child of Chinese immigrants, Maxine Hong Kingston had to learn to live in two different worlds. This was confusing for a young child, as she recalls in this selection from her autobiography, The Woman Warrior: Memoirs of a Girlhood Among Ghosts. *The immigrants regarded all non-Chinese as "ghosts"—pale, insubstantial,[1] and threatening.*

When I went to kindergarten and had to speak English for the first 1 time, I became silent. A dumbness—a shame—still cracks my voice in two, even when I want to say "hello" casually, or ask an easy question in front of the check-out counter, or ask directions of a bus driver. I stand frozen, or I hold up the line with a complete, grammatical sentence that comes squeaking out at impossible length. "What did you say?" says the cab driver or "Speak up," so I have to perform again, only weaker the second time. A telephone call makes my throat bleed and takes up the day's courage. It spoils my day with self-disgust when I hear my broken voice come skittering[2] out into the open. It makes people wince[3] to hear it. I'm getting better, though. Recently I asked the postman for special-issue stamps;[4] I've waited since childhood for postmen to give me some of their own accord.[5] I am making progress, a little every day.

My silence was thickest—total—during the three years that I covered 2 my school paintings with black paint. I painted layers of black over houses and flowers and suns, and when I drew on the blackboard, I put a layer of chalk on top. I was making a stage curtain, and it was the moment before the curtain parted or rose.[6] The teachers called my parents to school, and I saw they had been saving my pictures, curling and cracking, all alike and black. The teachers pointed to the pictures and looked serious, talked seriously too, but my parents did not understand English. ("In China, the par-

---

1 **insubstantial**   flimsy, without substance
2 **skittering**   rapidly and lightly, like a stone on top of water
3 **wince**   move without intention, like a person in pain
4 **special-issue stamps**   postal stamps of artistic design
5 **of their own accord**   voluntarily, without being asked
6 **rose**   from verb *rise,* go up

ABOUT THE AUTHOR
Maxine Hong Kingston, born in 1940, grew up in a Chinese immigrant community in Stockton, California, where her parents ran a laundry. She now lives in Hawaii and teaches writing at the University of Hawaii.

ents and teachers of criminals were executed,"[7] said my father.) My parents took the pictures home. I spread them out (so black and full of possibilities) and pretended the curtains were swinging open, flying up, one after another, sunlight underneath, mighty operas.

3   During the first silent year I spoke to no one at school, did not ask before going to the lavatory, and flunked kindergarten. My sister also said nothing for three years, silent in the playground and silent at lunch. There were other quiet Chinese girls not of our family, but most of them got over it sooner than we did. I enjoyed the silence. At first it did not occur to me I was supposed to talk or to pass kindergarten. I talked at home and to one or two of the Chinese kids in class. I made motions and even made some

---

7 **executed**   killed

171

jokes. I drank out of a toy saucer when the water spilled out of the cup, and everybody laughed, pointing at me, so I did it some more. I didn't know that Americans don't drink out of saucers... .

It was when I found out I had to talk that school became a misery, that the silence became a misery. I did not speak and felt bad each time that I did not speak. I read aloud in first grade, though, and heard the barest whisper with little squeaks come out of my throat. "Louder," said the teacher, who scared the voice away again. The other Chinese girls did not talk either, so I knew the silence had to do with being a Chinese girl. `4`

Reading out loud was easier than speaking because we did not have to make up[8] what to say, but I stopped often, and the teacher would think I'd gone quiet again. I could not understand "I." The Chinese "I" had seven strokes,[9] intricacies.[10] How could the American "I," assuredly wearing a hat like the Chinese, have only three strokes, the middle so straight? Was it out of politeness that this writer left off the strokes the way a Chinese has to write her own name small and crooked? No, it was not politeness; "I" is a capital and "you" is lower case. I stared at that middle line and waited so long for its black center to resolve into tight strokes and dots that I forgot to pronounce it. The other troublesome word was "here," no strong consonant to hang on to, and so flat, when "here" is two mountainous ideographs.[11] The teacher, who had already told me every day how to read "I" and "here" put me in the low corner under the stairs again, where the noisy boys usually sat. `5`

When my second grade class did a play, the whole class went to the auditorium except the Chinese girls. The teacher, lovely and Hawaiian, should have understood about us, but instead left us behind in the classroom. Our voices were too soft or nonexistent, and our parents never signed the permission slips anyway. They never signed anything unnecessary. We opened the door a crack and peeked out, but closed it again quickly. One of us (not me) won every spelling bee, though. `6`

I remember telling the Hawaiian teacher, "We Chinese can't sing 'land where our fathers died.'" She argued with me about politics, while I meant because of curses. But how can I have that memory when I couldn't talk. My mother says that we, like the ghosts, have no memories... . `7`

---

8 **make up** create, fabricate
9 **strokes** lines in Chinese writing
10 **intricacies** complexities
11 **ideographs** written symbols in Chinese

8. **Pair Work.** With a partner, decide what general conclusions you can draw from Kingston's details about herself. Write your ideas below.

READING STRATEGY: *Making Inferences* See page 252.

a. "A dumbness—a shame—still cracks my voice in two, even when I want to say 'hello' casually, or ask an easy question in front of the check-out counter, or ask directions of a bus driver." (Paragraph 1)

How do you think Kingston feels about speaking English?

_____

_____

b. "My silence was thickest—total—during the three years that I covered my school paintings with black paint. I painted layers of black over houses and flowers and suns, and when I drew on the blackboard, I put a layer of chalk on top. I was making a stage curtain, and it was the moment before the curtain parted or rose." (Paragraph 2)

In your opinion, what message was Kingston expressing through her art?

_____

_____

c. "The teachers called my parents to school, and I saw they had been saving my pictures, curling and cracking, all alike and black. The teachers pointed to the pictures and looked serious, talked seriously too, but my parents did not understand English. ('In China, the parents and teachers of criminals were executed,' said my father.)" (Paragraph 2)

What do you think her teachers were thinking? What do you think her parents were thinking?

_____

_____

_____

173

d. "I read aloud in first grade, though, and heard the barest whisper with little squeaks come out of my throat. 'Louder,' said the teacher, who scared the voice away again. The other Chinese girls did not talk either, so I knew the silence had to do with being a Chinese girl." (Paragraph 4)

How do you think the teacher interpreted Kingston's behavior in class? How do you interpret Kingston's behavior in class?

_____

_____

_____

When you finish, get together with two classmates to compare ideas.

READING STRATEGY:
Summarizing
See page 254.

9. **On your own.** Read the important ideas you underlined on pages 170–172 and make notes in the margin of ideas or words you might want to remember. Then, from your notes, write a brief summary below of Kingston's experience.

Summary of Kingston's experience:

_____

_____

_____

_____

When you finish, get together with a partner and take turns reading each other's summaries. Compare summaries. What is different? What is the same?

CRITICAL THINKING STRATEGY:
Analyzing
See page 258.

10. **Group Work.** Look at the reading on pages 170–172 with a writer's eye. As a child, Kingston had no voice in English; she says that even today she has trouble speaking English in public. Yet, she has a strong public voice as a writer of English.

List below some words Kingston uses to characterize herself as an English speaker. Then, choose phrases from Kingston's writing that you think show how good a writer she is. List them, too.

Kingston's "public" voice as an English speaker:

Example: silent

_____

_____

Kingston's voice as an English writer (our choices):

_____

_____

Ask one of your group to report several items from each list to the class.

11. **Group Work.** What connections can you make between TallMountain's poem and Kingston's essay? Have one person take notes for the group. The questions below might help you get started.

   • In the poem, what is the difference between the English world and the Athabaskan world? What other differences might you imagine?

   • In the essay, what is the difference between the English world and the Chinese world? What other differences might you imagine?

   • Think about the difficulty of moving from one world to the other. What difficulties does Kingston have? What difficulties does TallMountain have? How do their experiences compare to your own experience?

Working from notes, have one person in the group report your group's ideas to the class.

> **CRITICAL THINKING STRATEGY:**
> *Synthesizing*
> See page 263.

12. Writing Project. What experience with *two languages/two worlds* do you want to write about? Think of your classmates as your audience. The following suggestions might help you get started:

a. Do you remember the moment when you realized something important about speaking two languages? What happened? What did you realize? Make a note here of what you might want to focus on.

Possible focus:

_____

_____

WRITING STRATEGY:
Focusing Your Ideas
See page 239.

WRITING STRATEGY:
Quickwriting
See page 246.

Understanding Your Audience
See page 247.

Collecting Information
See page 238.

---

b. Quickwrite for five minutes in your journal, exploring your idea. See for yourself if this focus seems to work. If not, choose another idea and quickwrite about it.

c. Make a list of questions your classmates might want you to answer in your writing.

d. Make notes in your journal to prepare for writing this paper. Write down examples, quotations, and phrases you might use from the readings. Also, note what you remember from your own experience.

e. Drawing from your notes, write a first draft.

f. Ask a classmate or someone outside of class to read it and ask you questions about anything in the paper. From the questions, make notes in the margin for future work on the paper.

g. Place the draft in your writing folder.

CHAPTER FOUR

"Different Englishes"

READING STRATEGY:
Previewing
See page 253.

1. **Group Work.** Read the title of the article on page 180 and the italicized information below it. Then answer the questions below. Choose one person to take notes and report your group's ideas to the class.

   • What do you think the author, Amy Tan, means by "different Englishes"?

   • What might be special or unusual about her mother's English?

   • Why might "different Englishes" be important in Tan's life and in her writing?

CRITICAL THINKING
STRATEGY:
Analyzing
See page 258.

2. **Group Work.** Working together, study the three short dialogues below and answer the questions.

   a. *"Want other one spoon, Daddy."*
      "You mean, you want the other spoon."
      "Yes, I want other one spoon, please Daddy."
      "Can you say 'the other spoon'?"
      "Other…spoon. Now give me other one spoon?"

                    —George Yule, *The Study of Language*

   Who is speaking? What is their relationship to each other?

   _____

   How is one speaker's English different from the other's?

   _____

   b. *When my mother told me [I was going to take piano lessons], I felt as though I had been sent to hell. I whined and then kicked my foot a little when I couldn't stand it anymore.*

      "Why don't you like me the way I am? I'm not *a genius! I can't play the piano. And even if I could, I wouldn't go on TV if you paid me a million dollars!" I cried.*

My mother slapped me. "Who ask you be genius?" she shouted. "Only ask you be your best. For you sake. You think I want you be genius? Hnnh! What for! Who ask you!"

"So ungrateful," I heard her mutter in Chinese .

—Amy Tan, *The Joy Luck Club*

Who is speaking? What is their relationship?

_____

How is one speaker's English different from the other's?

_____

c. …*The American took several deep breaths, appearing to stare at the new mosque…. Then suddenly the man was charging ahead, toward the open doorway of the mosque.*

"No," Ahmed said. He dared to grab the American's arm.

" Please, it is not permitted."

"Rules were made to be bent." The big man puffed and winked.

"Not in Morocco."

"I'd like to go in there, kid."

"But it is not permitted."

"Why not? I'll take off my shoes."

"You are not of the faith."

"In Spain, they let anybody into mosques. What's so special here?"

Ahmed frowed, "I am very sorry. It is not so much what is special here as what is not special everywhere else."

The American shrugged. "Well, can't I even look in the door?"

—Tony Ardizzone, *Larabi's Ox*

Who is speaking? What is their relationship?

_____

How is one speaker's English different from the other's?

_____

Choose one person to report your group's ideas to the class.

3. **On your own.** Think of a time when you heard people speaking English in different ways. Quickwrite in your journal for five minutes about this experience. You might keep these questions in mind as you write:

   • Who were the speakers? What was the context?

   • How can you explain these differences?

   • When do you hear differences among speakers of your first language?

   • In either language, how might these differences cause conflict?

   Choose one or two ideas from your journal writing to share with the class.

WRITING STRATEGY:
Quickwriting
See page 246.

4. **On your own.** Quickly read through Amy Tan's essay on pages 180–183, without trying to "catch" it all. When you find an important idea, put a check (✓) in the margin. After you reach the end, go back to your check marks and make notes below about important ideas.

   Important ideas in Tan's essay:

   _____

   _____

   _____

   _____

   _____

   _____

   When you finish, compare notes with a partner to see if you selected some of the same ideas.

READING STRATEGY:
Scanning
See page 254.

5. **On your own.** Read the essay again—more slowly this time. As you read, make margin notes on ideas you think are important. When you finish, compare your margin notes to your notes in Activity 4. Revise your notes in Activity 4, if you have changed your mind.

READING STRATEGY:
Finding Main Ideas
See page 250.

Mother Tongue

by Amy Tan

from *Threepenny Review*

Fascinated by language in daily life, Amy Tan thinks a lot about the power of language—the way it can evoke a strong image, complex idea, or simple truth. In this selection, Tan talks about her mother's English and the importance of "different Englishes" in her own life and in her writing.

…Lately, I've been giving more thought to the kind of English my mother 1 speaks. Like others, I have described it to people as "broken" or "fractured" English. But I wince when I say that. It has always bothered me that I can think of no way to describe it other than "broken," as if it were damaged and needed to be fixed, as if it lacked a certain wholeness and soundness. I've heard other terms used, "limited English," for example. But they seem just as bad, as if every-thing is limited including people's perceptions[1] of the limited English speaker.

I know this for a fact, because when I was growing up, my mother's "lim- 2 ited" English limited my perception of her. I was ashamed of her English. I believed that her English reflected the quality of what she had to say. That is, because she expressed them imperfectly, her thoughts were imperfect. And I had plenty of empirical evidence to support me: the fact that people in depart-ment stores, at banks, and at restaurants did not take her seriously, did not give her good service, pretended not to understand her, or even acted as if they did not hear her.

My mother has long realized the limitations of her English as well. When 3 I was fifteen, she used to have me call people on the phone to pretend I was she. In this guise, I was forced to ask for information or even to complain and yell at people who had been rude to her. One time it was to call her stockbroker in New York. She had cashed out her small portfolio and it just so happened that we were going to go to New York the next week, our very first trip outside California. I had to get on the phone and say in an adolescent voice that was not very convincing, "This is Mrs. Tan."

And my mother was standing in the background, whispering loudly, "Why 4 he don't send me check, already two weeks late. So mad he lie to me, losing me money."

---

1 **perceptions**   insights, ideas

5   And then I said in perfect English, "Yes, I'm getting rather concerned. You agreed to send the check two weeks ago, but it hasn't arrived."

6   Then she began to talk more loudly, "What he want, I come to New York tell him front of his boss, you cheating me?" And I was trying to calm her down, make her be quiet, while telling the stockbroker, "I can't tolerate any more excuses. If I don't receive the check immediately, I am going to have to speak to your manager when I'm in New York next week." And sure enough, the following week there we were in front of this astonished[2] stockbroker, and I was sitting there red-faced and quiet, and my mother, the real Mrs. Tan, was shouting at his boss in her impeccable[3] broken English.

Amy Tan

7   We used a similar routine just five days ago, for a situation that was far less humorous. My mother had gone to the hospital for an appointment, to find out about a benign[4] brain tumor[5] a CAT scan[6] had revealed a month ago. She said she had spoken very good English, her best English, no mistakes. Still, she said, the hospital did not apologize when they said they had lost the CAT scan and she had come for nothing. She said they did not seem to have any sympathy when she told them she was anxious to know the exact diagnosis, since her husband and son had both died of brain tumors. She said they would not give her any more information until the next time and she would have to make another appointment for that. So she said she would not

---

2 **astonished**   surprised
3 **impeccable**   perfect
4 **benign**   not cancerous
5 **tumor**   growth
6 **CAT scan**   high technology (x-ray) picture

leave until the doctor called her daughter. She wouldn't budge. And when the doctor finally called her daughter, me, who spoke perfect English—lo and behold—we had assurances the CAT scan would be found, promises that a conference call on Monday would be held, and apologies for any suffering my mother had gone through for a most regrettable mistake.

I think my mother's English almost had an effect of limiting my possibilities in life as well. Sociologists and linguists probably will tell you that a person's developing language skills are more influenced by peers.[7] But I do think the language spoken in the family, especially in immigrant families, which are more insular,[8] plays a large role in shaping the language of the child, and I believe it affected my results on achievement tests, IQ test, and the SAT.[9] While my English skills were never judged as poor, English could not be considered my strong suit when compared to math. In grade school I did moderately well, getting perhaps B's, sometimes B-pluses, in English and scoring perhaps in the sixtieth or seventieth percentile on achievement tests. But those scores were not good enough to override the opinion that my abilities lay in math and science, because in those areas I achieved A's and scored in the ninetieth percentile or higher... . 8

I have been thinking about all this lately, about my mother's English, about achievement tests. Because lately I've been asked, as a writer, why there are not more Asian Americans represented in American literature. Why are there so few Asian Americans enrolled in creative writing programs? Why do so many Chinese students go into engineering? Well, these are broad sociological questions I can't begin to answer. But I have noticed in surveys—in fact, just last week—that Asian students, as a whole, do significantly better on math achievement tests than on English achievement tests. And this makes me think that there are other Asian-American students whose English spoken in the home might also be described as "broken" or "limited." And perhaps they also have teachers who are steering[10] them away from writing and into math and science, which is what happened to me. 9

Fortunately, I happen to be rebellious in nature and enjoy the challenge of disproving assumptions[11] made about me. I became an English major my first year in college, after being enrolled as pre-med. I started writing nonfiction as a free-lancer[12] the week after I was told by my former boss that writing was my worst skill and I should hone[13] my talents toward account management. 10

---

7 **peers** people of one's own age

8 **insular** isolated, separated from other people

9 **SAT** Scholastic Aptitude Test, often required for higher education

10 **steering** guiding

11 **assumptions** statements without proof

12 **free-lancer** writer who works independently, not employed by a firm

13 **hone** develop, perfect (v.), sharpen

11   But it wasn't until 1985 that I finally began to write fiction. And at first I wrote using what I thought to be wittily crafted[14] sentences, sentences that would finally prove that I had mastery over the English language. Here's an example from the first draft of a story that later made it into *The Joy Luck Club,* but without this line: "That was my mental quandary in its nascent state." A terrible line, which I can barely pronounce.

12   Fortunately, for reasons I won't go into today, I later decided I should envision a reader for the stories I would write. And the reader I decided upon was my mother, because these were stories about mothers. So with this reader in mind—and in fact she did read my early drafts—I began to write stories using all the Englishes I grew up with: the English I spoke to my mother, which for lack of a better term might be described as "broken"; my translation of her Chinese, which could certainly be described as "watered down" and what I imagined to be her translation of her Chinese if she could speak in perfect English, and for that I sought to preserve the essence,[15] but neither an English nor a Chinese structure. I wanted to capture what language ability tests can never reveal: her intent, her passion, her imagery, the rhythms of her speech, and the nature of her thoughts.

13   Apart from what any critic had to say about my writing, I knew I had succeeded where it counted when my mother finished reading my book and gave me her verdict: "So easy to read."

---

14 **wittily crafted**   cleverly written
15 **essence**   most important ingredient or property

ABOUT THE AUTHOR

Amy Tan was born in Oakland, California, in 1952, two and a half years after her parents immigrated to the United States. She is author of
The Joy Luck Club and *The Kitchen God's Wife.*

READING STRATEGY:
Using Context
See page 255.

6. **On your own.** Use context to guess the meanings of the under-lined words below. Circle the word or words that help you guess. Then compare ideas with a partner.

a. "…have described it [my mother's English] to people as 'broken' or '<u>fractured</u>' English. But I wince when I say that. It has always bothered me that I can think of no way to describe it other than 'broken,' as if it were damaged and needed to be fixed, as if it lacked a certain wholeness and soundness." (Paragraph 1)

My guess: _____

b. "I believed that her English reflected the quality of what she had to say. That is, because she expressed them imperfectly, her thoughts were imperfect. And I had plenty of <u>empirical evidence</u> to support me: the fact that people in department stores, at banks, and at restaurants did not take her seriously, did not give her good service, pretended not to understand her, or even acted as if they did not hear her." (Paragraph 2)

My guess: _____

c. "When I was fifteen, she used to have me call people on the phone to pretend I was she. In this <u>guise</u>, I was forced to ask for information or even to complain and yell at people who had been rude to her." (Paragraph 3)

My guess: _____

d. "So she said she would not leave until the doctor called her daughter. She wouldn't <u>budge</u>." (Paragraph 7)

My guess: _____

e. "While my English skills were never judged as poor, English could not be considered my <u>strong suit</u> when compared to math. …those [English] scores were not good enough to over-ride the opinion that my abilities lay in math and science, because in those areas I achieved A's and scored in the ninetieth percentile or higher… ." (Paragraph 8)

My guess: _____

7. **Group Work.** Have each person in the group choose a topic from the list below. Look back over the reading to refresh your memory and then tell what you know.

- Tell about Mrs. Tan's English from her adolescent daughter's point of view.

- Tell about Amy Tan's experience with tests.

- Tell about Amy Tan becoming a writer.

- Tell about the changes Tan made in her writing.

READING STRATEGY:
Paraphrasing
See page 253.

8. **On your own.** In the essay, Tan writes about her experience from her own point of view. Take an incident from the essay, with the viewpoint changed, and quickwrite about it in your journal for five minutes. One of the following might interest you:

- Tell about the "stockbroker" incident from the stockbroker's point of view.

- Tell about the "stockbroker" incident from Mrs. Tan's point of view.

- Tell about the hospital incident from the viewpoint of a member of the hospital staff.

Share an idea from your journal writing with the class.

WRITING STRATEGY:
Using Point of View
See page 247.

9. **On your own.** From your margin notes on pages 180–183 and from the notes you wrote in Activity 4, write a brief summary of *Mother Tongue.* Write it on a separate paper.

When you finish, get together with a classmate and read each other's summaries. What is different and what is the same?

READING STRATEGY:
Summarizing
See page 254.

10. **Pair Work.** Look at the essay on pages 180–183 with a writer's eye. Notice how Tan fills her writing with strong details to help the reader "see" what she means. For each general statement on the following page find details of support in the essay and note them in the chart.

CRITICAL THINKING STRATEGY:
Analyzing
See page 258.

Tan's generalizations:	Supporting details:
Tan's earlier perceptions of her mother were problematic.	Example: ashamed of her mother's English; thought her mother's thinking was imperfect if her mother's English was imperfect
Mrs. Tan realized the limitations of her English.	
Mrs. Tan was treated differently because of her English.	
Mrs. Tan's English almost limited her daughter's possibilities in life.	
There are not many Asian-American writers.	
Her mother played an important role in Amy Tan's development as a writer.	

Choose one example to share with the class.

11. Writing Project. What do you find interesting about Tan's experience? What lessons can others learn from Tan's experience? Which of Tan's conflicts concern you?

Among your ideas, find a topic to write about. In academic classes, teachers will often expect you to choose your own topic and relate it to the subject of the course.

a. For ideas related to language in conflict, look through your journal writing and the readings. What personal experience can you draw from? Make notes in your journal. As you narrow the possibilities, list your best ideas.

b. Choose the topic you like best and think of two or three important things you can say about this topic. These important points can become your focus. Write about these ideas for five minutes in your journal. See for yourself if this focus will work.

c. Use your journal as a place to "store" information and ideas. Look again for phrases, quotations, and examples from the readings in this unit. Include ideas and details from your own experience.

d. Decide who your audience is: Teachers? Parents? Friends? monolingual speakers of English? Educational administrators? Also, decide what you want to accomplish with your writing. Make notes of your ideas.

e. Drawing from your notes, write a first draft.

f. Ask someone outside of class to read the draft and ask you questions. From the questions, make notes in the margin for future work on the paper.

g. Place the draft in your writing folder.

> **WRITING STRATEGY:**
> **_Finding a Topic_**
> See page 239.
>
> **_Quickwriting_**
> See page 246.
>
> **_Collecting Information_**
> See page 238.
>
> **_Understanding Your Audience_**
> See page 247.

UNIT FOUR
Final Project

You now have four pieces of writing from Unit Four. Each is a rough draft—a collection of first ideas.

Choose one of these drafts to revise. It doesn't matter which one you choose, but you will probably want to choose the one that interests you most. As you draft and redraft your paper, ask yourself these questions:

To sharpen your focus

☑ Who are my readers?

☑ What is my focus? Is it limited enough?

☑ Which words are unnecessary? Which ones can I leave out?

To make your writing interesting

☑ How can I attract readers with my title?

☑ How can I "hook" readers with my introduction?

☑ Where can I add vivid details to "show" what I mean?

☑ Where can I work in a quotation or example?

☑ Can my readers "hear" my voice?

To help your readers follow your ideas

☑ What title will direct my readers to my topic?

☑ Does my introduction guide my readers?

☑ Can readers follow my ideas easily?

☑ Polishing Your Writing

Before you consider your last draft "finished," you'll want to polish your writing. Here are some suggestions:

1. **Vary sentence length.** If all of your sentences are short, your writing will seem "choppy." If all of your sentences are long, your readers will get tired. Look through your draft to find long sentences that you might break into short sentences or short sentences that you might combine.

Example:

Unpolished writing

During the first silent year I spoke to no one at school, did not ask before going to the lavatory, and flunked kindergarten, and my sister didn't say anything either, remaining silent in the playground and silent at lunch. There were other Chinese girls not of our family who got over it sooner than we did, but I enjoyed the silence.

Polished writing

During the first silent year I spoke to no one at school, did not ask before going to the lavatory, and flunked kindergarten. My sister also said nothing for three years, silent in the playground and silent at lunch. There were other quiet Chinese girls not of our family, but most of them got over it sooner than we did. I enjoyed the silence. (pg. 171)

2. **Connect your ideas.** Readers can follow your ideas better if you add words or phrases that connect your ideas. As you polish your writing, look for places where you can add a word or phrase to help your readers follow your thinking.

Example:

Unpolished writing

My family began to suspect I was having problems. I started school and my father says my early years in school were the worst years of his life. They weren't so good for me either. I can't find the words to express how bad it really was.

Polished writing

My family began to suspect I was having problems almost from the first day I started school. My father says my early years in school were the worst years of his life. They weren't so good for me, either. As I look back on it now, I can't find the words to express how bad it really was. (pg. 158)

3. **Check verb forms and verb tenses.** Incorrect grammar can confuse your readers. It can make them stop, go back, and start again. Readers don't like to do that. As you polish your writing, check all verb forms and tenses for accuracy.

Example:

Unpolished writing

One day a substitute teacher pick me to read aloud from the textbook. When I tell her, "No, thank you," she come unhinged. She think I was acting smart, and tell me so. I keep calm, and that get her madder and madder. We must have been spent 10 minutes try to solve the problem… .

Polished writing

One day a substitute teacher picked me to read aloud from the textbook. When I told her, "No, thank you," she came unhinged. She thought I was acting smart, and told me so. I kept calm, and that got her madder and madder. We must have spent 10 minutes trying to solve the problem… . (pg. 158)

4. **Check punctuation and spelling.** Readers pause at punctuation marks. If you have too many periods, commas, or semicolons, or you have them in the wrong places, you slow down and confuse your readers. Spelling errors also distract readers and slow them down. As you polish your writing, check your spelling and punctuation.

Example:

Unpolished writing

"The dying out of the language was partially our fault. Turtle said I speak Cherokee but I didnt tech it to me kids, now I use it more around the house."

Polished writing

"The dying out of the language was partially our fault," Turtle said. "I speak Cherokee, but I didn't teach it to my kinds. Now I use it more around the house." (pg. 150)

We asked an experienced writer to share her thoughts on polishing writing. Her is what she said:

Polishing Your Writing

On rare occasions, I get lucky. I've thought about what I want to say so much that all I need to do is "polish" my writing after I get my ideas down on paper. Usually, though, polishing is the last step after a lot of revising.

What's polishing? In jewelry-making, polishing is the final buffing[1] away of imperfections. The jeweler uses a soft cloth to smooth away rough edges. The jeweler rubs her jewelry until it shines. Until it's finished. Until it's as good as she can make it.

Imagine that you are a "writing jeweler." Where are those imperfections—those rough spots? If your writing were a silver ring, would it snag a cashmere sweater? Or, more to the point, would it irritate[2] your reader?

Everyone's polishing process is different. Mine involves a few tried-and-true[3] tricks of the trade.[4] First and foremost, I read my writing out loud. Many people, including myself, *hear* writing problems before they see them. Listen to your writing. When I stumble[5] over a sentence, I know to examine it carefully. Is it too long? Do I need to add a transition? Am I trying to use a voice or a word that isn't my own?

---

1 **buffing**   rubbing
2 **irritate**   bother, disturb
3 **tried-and-true**   shown to work well by repeated testing
4 **tricks of the trade**   special ways of doing things in a particular occupation or kind of work
5 **stumble**   miss a step, almost fall

I also read my writing out of order. Sometimes I even read an essay, sentence-by-sentence, backwards. Yes, backwards. Out-of-order reading is the easiest way I know to catch misspellings and simple grammatical errors.

Finally, I polish for "reader quirks."[6] Does my teacher, oftentimes my reader, have certain pet peeves?[7] Does Mr. Boyden dislike long paragraphs? I know that Dr. Murray hates it when her students forget to add a title. I try to remember my readers and revise for them.

After rereading the section I've just written, I'm contemplating a *real* title. "Polishing: Using a Soft Touch" might work well. Or how about "Polishing: The Art of the Writer's Craft"?

—*Amanda Buege*

---

6 **reader quirks**   a reader's odd likes and dislikes
7 **pet peeves**   strong dislikes

ABOUT THE AUTHOR
Amanda Buege, a native of St. Louis, Missouri (USA), writes and studies in New Orleans, Louisiana. With a friend and two cats, she lives on—literally *on*—the Mississippi River.

You, your classmates, and/or your teacher may want to use the following checklist to help you evaluate your writing:

Unit Four
Revising Checklist

	Yes ✓			
Sharpening your focus	**First draft**	**Second draft**	**Third draft**	**Final draft**
• Is it clear who the audience is?	❏	❏	❏	❏
• Is the topic limited enough?	❏	❏	❏	❏
• Have unnecessary words been deleted?	❏	❏	❏	❏
Making your writing interesting				
• Does the introduction "hook" the reader?	❏	❏	❏	❏
• Does the writer use interesting details?	❏	❏	❏	❏
• Does the writer's voice come through?	❏	❏	❏	❏
Helping your reader follow your ideas				
• Does the title suggest the writer's thinking?	❏	❏	❏	❏
• Does the introduction guide the reader?	❏	❏	❏	❏
• Can the reader perceive the writer's plan?	❏	❏	❏	❏
Polishing your ideas				
• Do the sentences vary in length?	❏	❏	❏	❏
• Are the ideas connected?	❏	❏	❏	❏
• Are the verb forms and tenses correct?	❏	❏	❏	❏
• Are the punctuation and spelling correct?	❏	❏	❏	❏

Your final draft may be placed in a class booklet, along with the drafts of your classmates. You can pass the booklet around for everyone to read.

UNIT FIVE
Relationships: Marriage

In this unit you will read four selections related to the theme of marriage.

- In your opinion, what are the advantages of being married?
- What are the disadvantages?

CHAPTER ONE

What Makes a Good Marriage?

1. **Group Work.** Read the title of the magazine article on page 198 and the definition of the word *bliss* below. Then answer the question that follows.

   bliss *n* complete happiness —**blissfully** *adv*

   In your opinion, what are the secrets of marital bliss? List your group's ideas.

   _____

   _____

   _____

   _____

   _____

   _____

   Compare lists with another group.

2. **On your own.** According to Madeline Drexler, the author of the article on pages 198–199, what is the secret of marital bliss? Read the first paragraph of the article to find her answer. Then complete the sentence below.

   According to Madeline Drexler, the secret of marital bliss is

   _____

   _____

   Compare ideas with your classmates.

3. **Class Work.** Drexler states the "secret of marital bliss" in the first paragraph of her article. What do you think she will write about in the rest of the article? What questions might she answer? Together brainstorm a list of questions and list them below.

READING STRATEGY:
Asking Questions
See page 249.

Questions	Answers

READING STRATEGY:
Reading for Specific Information
See page 254.

Finding Main Ideas
See page 250.

4. **On your own.** Read the article and look for answers to your questions from Activity 3. After you finish reading, share any answers you found with your classmates.

5. **On your own.** As you read the article a second time, underline the important ideas.

The Secrets of Marital Bliss

by Madeline Drexler

from the *Boston Globe Sunday Magazine*

*While some opposites may attract, researchers say, they
don't necessarily stick together for the long haul.*[1]

Sometimes, camouflaged[2] in the dense lingo of academia are the plain facts we need to run our lives. What, for instance, is the secret of a happy marriage? Not surprise gourmet meals, getaway weekends, or other nostrums[3] dispensed in women's magazines. Rather, according to one researcher, the secret of marital bliss resides in a simple notion: positive assortative mating. Translation: Marry someone like yourself.

Studies by Avshalom Caspi, associate professor of psychology at the University of Wisconsin, suggest that while some opposites may attract, they do not necessarily adhere.[4] Indeed, the glue that keeps people together is a common outlook[5] on life. Such romantic reciprocity begins early. It has long been known, for instance, that people tend to choose mates who have similar physical traits, intellect, and temperament.[6] The most stable partners, in other words, often have similar builds, read the same newspapers, and argue at the same decibel level. The tendency to seek mirror images doesn't stop at marriage; we also choose friends who are like us.

Why are we drawn to our own approximations?[7] "What we seek out are environments where we can feel comfortable to express who we are," Caspi says. Similarities set off romantic sparks, he says, because lonely singles "seek out a guarantee that there is a basis for interaction." Translation: a future together.

Sameness has even more profound effects in marriage. Having analyzed data from the 1930s to the 1950s in the longest study of married couples available, Caspi concluded that spouses who remained fairly similar in values and attitudes were more likely to stay together after 20 years; those who disagreed were more likely to split up. By values, Caspi meant religious and political beliefs and social and leisure pursuits. Attitudes encompassed opinions about marital fidelity,[8] premarital sex, child rearing, household manage-

---

1 **for the long haul**   forever
2 **camouflaged**   hidden
3 **nostrums**   popular cures
4 **adhere**   stick together

5 **outlook**   point of view
6 **temperament**   manner of thinking,
   behaving, and acting
7 **our own approximations**   people like us

ment, and the need for mates to hold common interests.

5   Longtime mates don't turn into clones[9] of each other. But, according to Caspi, they do tend to change in the same direction. Both, for instance, may be somewhat religious when they marry, though they may not practice the same religion. Years later, both will likely become more spiritual—or more agnostic. Whichever direction they take, they usually proceed in tandem,[10] as do their political paths and aesthetic journeys.

6   The cause of these parallel changes is not one partner's influence on the other. Rather, it is shared experience. Researchers use an unwitting pun to describe the phenomenon, "mutual niche picking." Translation: Spouses often like to do the same things. Bringing up kids together, trekking to the beach every summer, and going to the same parties reinforce common values. These shared experiences in turn strengthen the marriage. As Caspi sees it, the phenomenon is circular: Similar partners choose each other, then pursue similar directions during their marriage, causing them to share experiences and thus sustain their similarities. Similar spouses are also more likely to be friendly to each other and happy in their marriages, perhaps because they demand less from mates and don't have to change themselves.

7   To be sure, some experts disagree with Caspi. John Gottman, professor of psychology at the University of Washington, says it is not similarity that helps spouses stay together but being able to handle differences. "They need to have the same style of dealing with conflict," Gottman says.

8   Still, Caspi and others contend that a union of opposites is not necessarily a match made in heaven.[11] Take the Prince and Princess of Wales. "There was a good deal of dissimilarity from the outset," Caspi observes. "Did she ever play polo? Did she care about his obsession with bad architecture? Did he take an interest in her social concerns?"

9   As Caspi expressed it in a more academic context: "Spouse similarity covaries with relationship satisfaction." Translation: Don't fall in love with a cowboy if horses make you sneeze.

---

8 **fidelity**   faithfulness
9 **clones**   duplicates; copies
10 **in tandem**   together
11 **match made in heaven**   a very good match

6. On your own. Choose the correct form of the word to complete the sentences below. Make any necessary changes in the form and tense of the verbs. Then compare sentences with a classmate.

Noun	Verb	Adjective	Adverb
necessity	necessitate	necessary	necessarily
attraction	attract	attractive	attractively
reciprocity	reciprocate	reciprocal	reciprocally
interaction	interact	interactive	interactively
analysis	analyze	analytical	analytically

a. It is not _____ to become a clone of your

spouse in order to have a successful marriage.

b. John Gottman says that being able to handle differences is a

_____ if a marriage is going to succeed.

c. Caspi believes that we are _____ to people

like ourselves because it provides a comfortable environment in

which we can express ourselves honestly and openly.

d. What qualities in a person are _____ to you?

e. He expressed interest in getting to know her better, but she did

not _____ .

f. If there is little _____ between partners, they

are unlikely to sustain their similarities.

g. Caspi's _____ of married couples used data

from the 1930s to the 1950s.

h. Researchers do not always come up with the same results when

they _____ the data.

7. **On your own.** What is the main idea of each paragraph in the article on pages 198–199? Restate these ideas in your own words.

READING STRATEGY:
Finding Main Ideas
See page 250.

Paragraph	Main Idea
1	The secret of happiness in marriage is to marry someone like yourself.
2	
3	
4	
5	
6	
7	
8	
9	

Compare ideas with your classmates.

▪◦‖◇‖◦▪‖◦‖◇‖◦▪‖◦‖◇‖◦▪

WRITING STRATEGY:
Quickwriting
See page 246.

8. On your own. Choose one of the main ideas in your chart from Activity 7. For five to ten minutes, quickwrite about this idea. Here are some questions you can think about as you write:

• What do you find interesting about this idea?

• Do you agree or disagree with this idea? Why?

• Does this idea make you think of anything or anyone from your own experience?

▪◦‖◇‖◦▪‖◦‖◇‖◦▪‖◦‖◇‖◦▪

WRITING STRATEGY:
Using Quotations
See page 248.

9. Pair Work. Who does Drexler quote in her article? Collect information about these people in the chart below. Then answer the questions that follow.

Name	Credentials	Position on the topic

a. Why does she quote these people?

b. Why do you think she mentions their credentials?

Get together with another pair of students and compare ideas.

10. **Pair Work.** In the 6th paragraph, the writer describes a chain of events. One event causes something to happen which in turn causes something else to happen. Describe this chain of events in the chart below.

> **CRITICAL THINKING STRATEGY:** *Analyzing* See page 258.

Cause	Effect
People choose partners like themselves.	
Partners have shared experiences.	
Partners remain alike.	

Compare charts with another pair of students.

11. **Pair Work.** Reread the last paragraph of the article. Together think of another way to translate Caspi's idea.

As Caspi expressed it in a more academic context: "Spouse similarity covaries with relationship satisfaction."

Translation:

_____

_____

Share ideas with your classmates.

12. **Class Work.** List several examples of academic language from the article. Based on these examples, how would you describe academic language? List the characteristics. Then answer the questions below.

> **CRITICAL THINKING STRATEGY:** *Analyzing* See page 258.

Examples of academic language:

Spouse similarity covaries with relationship satisfaction.

_____

_____

Characteristics of academic language:

_____

_____

a. Why do you think Drexler translates the examples of academic language?

b. What does this tell you about her audience?

c. How would this article be different if she were writing for a psychology journal?

Share ideas with your classmates.

13. **Writing Project.** According to Avshalom Caspi, the secret to happiness in marriage is to marry someone like yourself. Explore this idea by describing a married couple you know well. Tell how these two people are the same and different. Then decide if you think this couple supports Caspi's thesis. Here are some suggestions to help you get started:

   a. Choose a married couple to write about. Compare and contrast these two people and record your ideas in a Venn Diagram. In the center area of the diagram, tell how these two people are alike. In the outer areas, tell how they are different. As you look for similarities and differences, consider how you would describe each person's physical traits, temperament, interests, values, and attitudes.

WRITING STRATEGY:
*Making a
Venn Diagram*
See page 244.

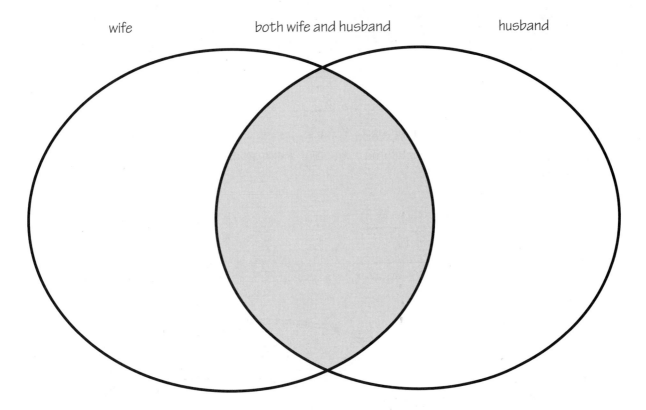

wife   both wife and husband   husband

b. Describe this couple to a classmate, stressing the similarities or differences that you think are important. Listen to any ideas or questions that your classmate has.

c. Decide if you think this couple supports Caspi's thesis. Note your reasons why or why not.

d. Decide which ideas you want to include in your writing. Then consider how you might organize these ideas.

e. Quickwrite in your journal for five minutes, experimenting with different ways to begin your paper. Remember that your introduction needs to catch your readers' attention and show the direction your writing will take.

f. Write a first draft of your paper.

g. Read Around. Get together with a group of classmates. Take turns reading each other's papers.

h. Place a copy of your writing in your writing folder.

WRITING STRATEGY:
Organizing Ideas
See page 245.

CHAPTER TWO

What Is Marriage?

WRITING STRATEGY:
Making a Cluster Diagram
See page 241.

1. **Class Work.** Think about the word *marriage* and write any ideas that come to mind on a cluster diagram on the board.

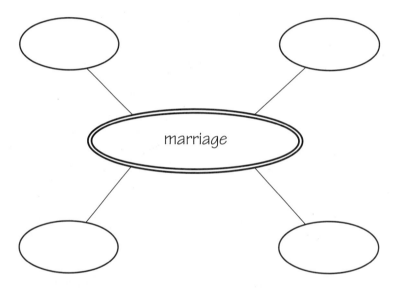

Choose a word or phrase from your cluster diagram and quickwrite in response to it.

READING STRATEGY:
Predicting
See page 253.

2. **Class Work.** The title of the poem on the next page is simply *On Marriage.* How might the poet focus his ideas on marriage? List some of the possibilities.

   Example: *the advantages of getting married*

3. **Pair Work.** Listen as your teacher reads this poem aloud. Then get together with a partner and take turns reading it aloud.

On Marriage

by Kahlil Gibran

Love one another, but make not a bond of love:
Let it rather be a moving sea between the shores of your souls.
Fill each other's cup, but drink not from one cup.
Give one another of your bread, but eat not from the same loaf.
Sing together and be joyous, but let each one of you be alone,
Even as the strings of the lute are alone,
Though they quiver with the same music.
Give your hearts, but not into each other's keeping,
For only the land of life can contain your hearts.
Stand together, yet not too near together.
For the pillars of the temple stand apart,
And the oak tree and the cyprus grow not in each other's shade.

4. **Class Work.** Which words in the poem are unfamilar to you? List them on the board. Then use these strategies to learn the meanings of these words:

   • Try to guess the meaning from context.

   • See if any of your classmates know the meaning of the words.

   • Look up the words in a dictionary.

5. **On your own.** Choose a line or sentence from the poem that interests you and think about it for several minutes. In your journal, write down any ideas that come to mind.

CRITICAL THINKING
STRATEGY:
Interpreting
See page 262.

6. **Group Work.** There are seven sentences in this poem. Tell what each sentence means to you and record your group's ideas in the chart below.

Sentence	Our interpetation
1	
2	
3	
4	
5	
6	
7	

Share your group's ideas with the class.

7. **Class Work.** Listen as your teacher reads the poem on page 209 aloud.

(Untitled)

Judith Viorst

On the way home with my husband from the dinner party,
I thought I'd very tactfully point out
That he shouldn't interrupt, and that
He shouldn't talk with his hands, and that
He shouldn't, when discussing politics, shout.
And that he shouldn't tell that story while people
      are eating, and that
He shouldn't tell that joke for the rest of his
      life, and that
He shouldn't have said what he said about that
      terrible lady in red because
She happens to be the-person-he said-it-to's wife.
And that he didn't need that second helping of
      mousse cake, and that
He didn't need to finish the Chardonnay.
But after thirty years of marriage
I finally understand what not to say
On the way home with my husband from a
      dinner party.

CRITICAL THINKING
STRATEGY:
Interpreting
See page 262.

8. **Group Work.** Choose two of these questions to discuss. Have one person in your group take notes on your discussion.

   a. Based on the ideas in the poem, what general advice do you think the narrator would give a newly married couple? Is this good advice? Why or why not?

   b. Why doesn't the narrator tell her husband what is on her mind? What do you think would happen if she did?

   c. What would be a good title for this poem?

   d. Imagine that you are the narrator's husband. What are you thinking about on the way home from the dinner party?

   Share your group's ideas with the class.

9. **Pair Work.** Write a short dialogue between two married people who are driving home from a dinner party. You might begin your dialogue with one of the lines below.

   "You shouldn't shout when you are discussing politics."
   "I wish you wouldn't tell that awful story while people are eating."
   "Why did you tell that stupid joke?"
   "You really shouldn't have eaten that second helping of mousse cake."

   When you have finished writing, read your dialogue to your class-mates.

CRITICAL THINKING
STRATEGY:
Synthesizing
See page 263.

10. **Group Work.** Look for a connection between the ideas in the Drexler article on pages 198–199 and one or both of the poems in this chapter (pages 207 and 209). Choose one person in your group to take notes. Then share your group's ideas with the class.

11. **Writing Project.** In writing, explore your ideas about marriage. Although no simple definition of marriage is possible, what key ideas do you think best explain what marriage is, or is supposed to be? The following suggestions might help you as you write.

a. Look back over the readings and activities in Chapters 1 and 2 of this unit. Collect the ideas that you might want to use in your writing, making sure to keep track of your sources.

b. With several classmates, brainstorm a set of questions about marriage. Decide if you want to answer any of these questions in your writing.

c. Try quickwriting to complete the sentences below. Then share ideas with a classmate.

Marriage is

_____

_____

The best thing about being married is

_____

_____

The worst thing about being married is

_____

_____

I want/don't want to be married because

_____

_____

> **WRITING STRATEGY:**
> *Collecting Information*
> See page 238.

d. Think about how the authors in these chapters focused their writing. Then look back over your notes and choose a focus for your writing. Choose a focus that you can explore in depth in a two- to three-page paper.

e. Identify your audience. Think about what they already know about your topic and what they might be interested in reading about.

f. Collect details and examples to illustrate your ideas. Then tell a partner what you are planning to write about. Listen to any questions that your partner has.

g. Write a first draft of your paper.

h. Place a copy of your paper in your writing folder.

> **WRITING STRATEGY:**
> *Focusing Your Ideas*
> See page 239.
>
> *Understanding Your Audience*
> See page 247.

CHAPTER THREE

What Pulls Couples Apart?

1. **Group Work.** Read the title of the newspaper article on page 214. What do you think are "the forces" that pull couples apart? In other words, what might cause a couple to separate or divorce? Share ideas and record them in your journal.

CRITICAL THINKING
STRATEGY:
Synthesizing
See page 263.

2. **Group Work.** Think back to the other readings in this unit. What do you think Caspi, Gibran, and Viorst would say pulls couples apart? Share ideas and then write them on the lines below.

What pulls couples apart?

Avshalom Caspi might say:

_____

_____

_____

Khalil Gibran might say:

_____

_____

_____

Judith Viorst might say:

_____

_____

_____

3. **Class Work.** The sentence below is from the newspaper article on pages 214–216. Read the sentence and follow the instructions below.

> "…the latest studies suggest that the marriages most likely to dissolve are those in which some or all of these four behaviors are chronic: criticism, contempt, defensiveness and withdrawal."

Read the four quotations below. Decide if the quotation is an example of criticism, contempt, defensiveness, or withdrawal.

a. "I don't want to talk about it."

_____

b. "You're too dumb to understand."

_____

c. "You shouldn't talk with your hands."

_____

d. "How can you say I don't listen to you? I do."

_____

CRITICAL THINKING STRATEGY:
Interpreting
See page 262.

4. **On your own.** As you read the article, underline the important ideas. In the margin, write down any thoughts and questions that come to mind.

READING STRATEGY:
Finding Main Ideas
See page 250.

Resisting the Forces That Pull Couples Apart

by Alison Bass

from *The Boston Globe*

For the first time, researchers are arriving at a consensus[1] on what it 1
takes for a marriage to survive. Like the ingredients of successful marriages
themselves, the findings are often surprising.

There is now strong evidence, for example, that the relationships most 2
likely to end in divorce are not necessarily those in which spouses fight,
passionately or often. Nor are married couples who have agreed to avoid
conflict invariably headed for trouble, as previous research had suggested.

Rather, the latest studies suggest that the marriages most likely to dis- 3
solve are those in which some or all of these four behaviors are chronic:[2]
criticism, contempt, defensiveness and withdrawal. Psychologist John
Gottman, along with several other respected researchers in the field, have
found that they are the strongest predictors of separation and divorce.

"It's not the amount of empathy or understanding in a relationship that 4
predicts who is going to make it and who is going to divorce," says Howard
Markman, professsor of psychology at the University of Denver. "It's the
zingers[3] or negative behaviors that are far more predictive over time. As we
say, one zinger erases 20 positive acts of kindness."

"The basic finding is that anger and disagreement are not harmful to a 5
marriage; it's when that anger is blended with contempt and defensiveness
that it's very destructive," agrees Gottman, professor of psychology at the
University of Washington in Seattle.

In separate but parallel investigations, Markman and Gottman have 6
conducted long-term studies of married couples for more than 10 years.

---

1 **consensus** agreement
2 **chronic** constant, lasting a long time
3 **zingers** hurtful remarks

While much previous research on marriages has been anecdotal[4] and sometimes contradictory, the new findings by Gottman and Markman and others are unusually consistent.

7   Many researchers, for example, agree that it is typically the wife who takes emotional responsibility for the status of the marriage. She is most often the one who brings up the thorny[5] issues that need to be negotiated and resolved if the marriage is to succeed, and she is the one who persists until the discussion ends in a satisfactory resolution or a screaming match.[6]

8   It is when the wife gives up the role of emotional caretaker and withdraws, typically after years of destructive conflict, that many marriages hit rock bottom.[7]

9   "Once the woman gives up, that's when she's likely to file for divorce or have an affair,"[8] Markman says. "And many men have no clue as to how bad things have got until they get the letter about divorce."

10   Husbands and men in general are much more uncomfortable with conflict in relationships and thus more likely to withdraw from a potential argument, either by placating[9] their wives, even though they might be steaming inside, or by stonewalling—becoming silent and disengaged. Typical in this scenario is the husband who turns on the television or walks out of the room.

11   Both Markman and Gottman found that consistent withdrawal or stonewalling by the husband is strongly predictive of divorce.

12   Conversely, constant criticism or contempt on the part of the wife is also predictive of marital distress and divorce. It often leads to a vicious cycle: The wife criticizes or blames the husband, the husband becomes defensive and either withdraws from the discussion or defends himself by going on the attack. The result is a highly destructive fight that can end in verbal and physical abuse.

13   The good news is that these patterns can be changed once spouses recognize the role each plays in creating them and learn how to communicate more effectively.

14   Markman tells the story of Leslie and Michael, who had been married for 14 years and were deeply discouraged about their relationship. Leslie is what Markman calls a pursuer. When she is troubled by some aspect of the relationship, she attempts to talk about it with Michael. Michael per-

---

4 **anecdotal**   based on personal stories
5 **thorny** difficult
6 **screaming match**   loud fight
7 **rock bottom**   lowest point
8 **have an affair**   have sexual relations outside the marriage
9 **placating** yielding to, giving in to

ceives problems as well but is less likely to bring them up. He would rather live with what he considers minor disappointments than risk a big argument. But when Leslie brings up an issue, Michael treats it as "no big deal"—dismissing her concerns—or he gets defensive and recites a litany of all the things she has done wrong.

Through counseling,[10] Leslie and Michael were able to alter this well-worn script. "We showed Leslie how to present her concerns, gripes[11] or disappointments in such a way that she...would be heard," Markman says. "With Michael, we concentrated on developing his listening skills so he could accurately detect and appreciate Leslie's concerns." 15

Perhaps the most critical task of a marriage, researchers agree, is forging[12] a shared style of communication that honors both partners' need for love and respect. And fortunately, there is more than one workable style for happy marriages. 16

---

10 **counseling**   advice from a psychologist or other person trained to help people solve their problems
11 **gripes**   complaints
12 **forging**   building

216

5. On your own. Use context to guess the meaning of the <u>underlined</u> words below. Underline the word or words that help you to guess. Then compare ideas with your classmates.

READING STRATEGY:
Using Context
See page 255.

a. "'It's not the amount of <u>empathy</u> or understanding in a relation-ship that predicts who is going to make it and who is going to divorce,' says Howard Markman, professor of psychology at the University of Denver."

My guess: _____

b. "'The basic finding is that anger and disagreement are not harmful to a marriage; it's when that anger is <u>blended with</u> contempt and defensiveness that it's very destructive,'... ."

My guess: _____

c. "In separate but <u>parallel</u> investigations, Markman and Gottman have conducted long-term studies of married couples for more than 10 years. While much previous research on marriages has been anecdotal and sometimes contradictory, the new findings by Gottman and Markman and others are unusually <u>consistent</u>."

My guess: _____

My guess: _____

d. "Many researchers, for example, agree that it is typically the wife who takes emotional responsibility for the status of the mar-riage. She is most often the one who brings up the thorny issues that need to be negotiated and resolved if the marriage is to succeed, and she is the one who persists until the discus-sion ends in a satisfactory <u>resolution</u> or a screaming match."

My guess: _____

e. "Husbands and men in general are much more uncomfortable with conflict in relationships and thus more likely to withdraw from a potential argument, either by placating their wives, even though they might be <u>steaming</u> inside, or by <u>stonewalling</u>— becoming silent and disengaged."

My guess: _____

My guess: _____

6. **On your own.** Choose the correct form of the word to complete the sentences below. Make any necessary changes in the form and tense of the verbs.

Noun	Verb	Adjective	Adverb
criticism	criticize	critical	critically
predictor	predict	predictive	
prediction			
empathy	empathize	empathetic	empathetically
defensiveness		defensive	defensively
contradiction	contradict	contradictory	
destruction	destroy	destructive	destructively

a. Instead of _____ his wife on the way home from the dinner party, he kept silent.

b. It is difficult to be around someone who is always speaking

_____ .

c. Markman and Gottman use negative behaviors to

_____ which marriages will fail. Their

_____ are often accurate.

d. Couples who can _____ with each other are not necessarily going to have a successful marriage. However, it

helps to be _____ .

218

e. "What do you mean I don't listen to you? I do." he responded

_____ . This kind of _____

did not help their marriage.

f. In some ways, the research findings of Markman and Gottman

and the research findings of Caspi are _____ .

g. According to Markman and Gottman, the "zingers" can

_____ a marriage.

h. Certain types of behavior are very _____ to
marriages.

Compare answers with your classmates.

7. **On your own.** This article presents the findings of two
researchers—John Gottman and Howard Markman. Choose what
you think are the three most important research findings. Restate
them below in your own words.

READING STRATEGY:
Paraphrasing
See page 253.

_____

_____

_____

Share ideas with your classmates.

8. **Pair Work.** According to the article, how do these actions or behaviors affect a marriage? State your answers in your own words. Then compare ideas with your classmates.

zingers   *It's the zingers that cause a marriage to*

_____
                 fail.

acts of kindness _____

_____

_____

219

fighting passionately _____

_____

stonewalling _____

_____

communicating _____

_____

CRITICAL THINKING
STRATEGY:
Comparing
See page 260.

9. **Pair Work.** What are the ingredients of a successful marriage? Compare the ideas of the people in the chart below. Then add your own ideas.

Ingredients of a successful marriage

Avashalom Caspi	
Kahil Gibran	
Judith Viorst	
Gottman and Markman	

My partner	
Me	

What similarities and differences did you find? Share ideas with another pair.

Caspi and Gibran both think that… .

According to both Caspi and Gibran,… .

Caspi thinks that…, but Gottman and Markman believe that… .

10. **Writing Assignment.** In writing, respond to one of the quotations below. Use ideas and information from the readings in this unit as well as from your own experience.

"When a match has equal partners / then I fear not."
   —Aeschylus *(Greek playwright, 525–456 B.C.)*

"Happiness in marriage is entirely a matter of chance."
   —Jane Austen *(English novelist, 1775–1817)*

"Chains do not hold a marriage together. It is threads, hundreds of tiny threads, which sew people together through the years."
   —Simone Signoret *(French actress, 1921–1985)*

"The best part about married life is the fights. The rest is merely so-so."
   —Thornton Wilder *(American novelist and playwright, 1897–1975)*

Here are some suggestions to help you get started:

▨▨▥◇▨▦▩◇▨▥◇▨▩▦▩◇

CRITICAL THINKING STRATEGY:
Interpreting
See page 262.

▨▥◇▨▦▥◇▨▦▥◇▨▦▥◇

WRITING STRATEGY:
Quickwriting
See page 246.

a. Get together with several classmates to discuss each quotation. Tell what each quotation means to you and if you agree with it.

b. Choose the quotation that interests you the most. For five to ten minutes quickwrite in response to the quotation. Then look over your quickwriting to find one or two key ideas that you might develop in a longer piece of writing.

c. Look back over the articles and poems in this unit to find ideas and information that either support or refute the ideas in the quotation. Be sure to cite your source when you take notes.

d. Think about how you might organize your writing.

e. Write a first draft of your paper.

f. Place a copy of your writing in your writing folder.

CHAPTER FOUR

Who Should You Marry?

1. **Journal Writing.** Did anyone ever give you advice about marriage? What did they say? How did you feel about the advice then? How do you feel about this advice now? Explore these questions as you write in your journal.

2. **Class Work.** The lines below are from the short story on pages 225–228. Given the theme of this unit, what do you think the missing words might be? Brainstorm a set of possibilities.

   My grandmother gave me bad advice and good advice when I was in my early teens. For the bad advice, she said that

   _____ . *For the good advice, she said that*

   _____ .

> ▓░▓░▓░▓░▓░▓░▓░
>
> **READING STRATEGY:**
> *Previewing*
> See page 253.

   Scan the first paragraph of the story to find the grandmother's advice. How do you think Avshalom Caspi, cited in the article on pages 198–199, would respond to this advice? Share ideas and record them in your journal.

> ▓░▓░▓░▓░▓░▓░▓░
>
> **READING STRATEGY:**
> *Scanning*
> See page 254.

3. **On your own.** Read the first paragraph of the story. What information do you get about the narrator and his grandmother in this part of the story? List this information on the lines below.

Narrator	Narrator's grandmother
doesn't live with his grandmother	*speaks Spanish*

READING STRATEGY:
Making Inferences
See page 252.

Based on this information, what inferences can you make about the narrator and his grandmother? Share ideas with your classmates.

Inferences about the narrator:

_____

_____

_____

Inferences about the narrator's grandmother:

_____

_____

_____

4. **On your own.** As you read the rest of the story, try these strategies to read actively:

READING STRATEGY:
Asking Questions
See page 249.

• Ask yourself questions as you read.

   Examples:

   Why did the writer include this information?

   Why do the characters act in this way? What would I do?

• Make predictions as you read. Stop reading occasionally and think about what might happen next in the story.

• Stop reading at different points in the story and summarize what you have read.

Like Mexicans

by Gary Soto

1   My grandmother gave me bad advice and good advice when I was in my early teens. For the bad advice, she said that I should become a barber because they made good money and listened to the radio all day. "Honey, they don't work como burros," she would say every time I visited her. She made the sound of donkeys braying. "Like that, honey!" For the good advice, she said that I should marry a Mexican girl. "No Okies, hijo"—she would say—"Look my son. He marry one and they fight every day about I don't know what and I don't know what." For her, everyone who wasn't Mexican, black, or Asian were Okies. The French were Okies, the Italians in suits were Okies. When I asked about Jews, whom I had read about, she asked for a picture. I rode home on my bicycle and returned with a calendar depicting the important races of the world. "Pues se, son Okies tambien!" she said, nodding her head. She saved the calendar away and we went to the living room where she lectured me on the virtues of the Mexican girl: first, she could cook and, second, she acted like a woman, not a man, in her husband's home. She said she would tell me about a third when I got a little older.

2   I asked my mother about it—becoming a barber and marrying Mexican. She was in the kitchen. Steam curled from a pot of boiling beans, the radio was on, looking as squat as a loaf of bread. "Well, if you want to be a barber—they say they make good money." She slapped a round steak with a knife, her glasses slipping down with each strike. She stopped and looked up. "If you find a good Mexican girl, marry her of course." She returned to slapping the meat and I went to the backyard where my brother and David King were sitting on the lawn.

3   I ignored them and climbed the back fence to see my best friend, Scott, a second-generation Okie. I called him and his mother pointed to the side of the house where his bedroom was a small aluminum trailer,[1] the kind you gawk at when they're flipped over on the freeway, wheels spinning in the air. I went around to find Scott pitching horseshoes.[2]

---

1 **trailer**   mobile home
2 **pitching horseshoes**   a game in which horseshoes are tossed at a stake

I picked up a set of rusty ones and joined him. While we played, we 4 talked about school and friends and record albums. The horseshoes scuffed up dirt, sometimes ringing the iron that threw out a meager shadow like a sundial. After three argued-over games, we pulled two oranges apiece from his tree and started down the alley[3] still talking school and friends and record albums. We pulled more oranges from the alley and talked about who we would marry. "No offense,[4] Scott," I said with an orange slice in my mouth, "but I would *never* marry an Okie." We walked in step, almost touching, with a sled of shadows dragging behind us. "No offense, Gary," Scott said, "but I would never marry a Mexican." I looked at him: a fang of orange slice showed from his munching mouth. I didn't think anything of it. He had his girl and I had mine. But our seventh-grade vision was the same: to marry, get jobs, buy cars and maybe a house if we had money left over.

We talked about our future lives until, to our surprise, we were on the 5 downtown mall,[5] two miles from home. We bought a bag of popcorn at Penneys and sat on a bench near the fountain watching Mexican and Okie girls pass. "That one's mine," I pointed with my chin when a girl with eyebrows arched into black rainbows ambled by. "She's cute," Scott said about a girl with yellow hair and a mouthful of gum. We dreamed aloud, our chins busy pointing out girls. We agreed that we couldn't wait to become men and lift them onto our laps.

But the woman I married was not Mexican but Japanese. It was a sur- 6 prise to me. I went about wide-eyed in my search for the brown girl in a white dress at a dance. I searched the playground at the baseball diamond. When the girls raced for grounders,[6] their hair bounced like something that couldn't be caught. When they sat together in the lunchroom, heads pressed together, I knew they were talking about us Mexican guys. I saw them and dreamed them. I threw my face into my pillow, making up sentences that were good as in the movies.

But when I was twenty, I fell in love with this other girl who worried my 7 mother, who had my grandmother asking once again to see the calendar of the Important Races of the World. I told her I had thrown it away years before. I took a much-glanced-at snapshot from my wallet. We looked at it together, in silence. Then grandma reclined in her chair, lit a cigarette, and said, "Es pretty." She blew and asked with all her worry pushed up to her forehead: "Chinese?"

---

3 **alley**   narrow street
4 **No offense**   Don't be offended.
5 **mall**   large open area for pedestrians
6 **grounders**   in baseball, batted balls that roll along the ground

226

8   I was in love and there was no looking back. She was the one. I told my mother who was slapping hamburger into patties. "Well, sure if you want to marry her," she said. But the more I talked, the more concerned she became. Later I began to worry. Was it all a mistake? "Marry a Mexican girl," I heard my mother say in my mind. I heard it at breakfast. I heard it over math problems, between Western Civilization and cultural geography. But then one afternoon while I was hitchhiking home from school, it struck me[7] like a baseball in the back: my mother wanted me to marry someone of my own social class—a poor girl. I considered my fiancee, Carolyn, and she didn't look poor, though I knew she came from a family of farm workers and pull-yourself-up-by-your-bootstraps[8] ranchers. I asked my brother, who was marrying Mexican poor that fall, if I should marry a poor girl. He screamed "Yeah" above his terrible guitar playing in his bedroom. I considered my sister who had married Mexican. Cousins were dating Mexican. Uncles were marrying poor women. I asked Scott, who was still my best friend, and he said, "She's too good for you, so you better not."

9   I worried about it until Carolyn took me home to meet her parents. We drove in her Plymouth until the houses gave way to[9] farms and ranches and finally her house fifty feet from the highway. When we pulled into the drive, I panicked and begged Carolyn to make a U-turn and go back so we could talk about it over a soda. She pinched my cheek, calling me a "silly boy." I felt better, though, when I got out of the car and saw the house: the chipped paint, a cracked window, boards for a walk to the back door. There were rusting cars near the barn. A tractor with a net of spiderwebs under a mulberry. A field. A bale of barbed wire like children's scribbling leaning against an empty chicken coop. Carolyn took my hand and pulled me to my future mother-in-law who was coming out to greet us.

10   We had lunch: sandwiches, potato chips, and iced tea. Carolyn and her mother talked mostly about neighbors and the congregation[10] at the Japanese Methodist Church in West Fresno. Her father, who was in khaki work clothes, excused himself with a wave that was almost a salute and went outside. I heard a truck start, a dog bark, and then the truck rattle away.

11   Carolyn's mother offered another sandwich, but I declined with a shake of my head and a smile. I looked around when I could, when I was not saying over and over that I was a college student, hinting that I could take care of her daughter. I shifted my chair. I saw newspapers piled in corners, dusty

---

7   **struck me**   occurred to me

8   **pull-yourself-up-by-your-bootstraps**   become successful without the help of others

9   **gave way to**   were replaced by

10   **congregation**   people who belong to a church

cereal boxes and vinegar bottles in corners. The wallpaper was bubbled from rain that had come in from a bad roof. Dust. Dust lay on lamp shades and window sills. The people are just like Mexicans, I thought. Poor people.

Carolyn's mother asked me through Carolyn if I would like a *sushi*. A plate of black and white things were held in front of me. I took one, wide-eyed, and turned it over like a foreign coin. I was biting into one when I saw a kitten crawl up the window screen over the sink. I chewed and the kitten opened its mouth of terror as she crawled higher, wanting in to paw the leftovers from our plates. I looked at Carolyn who said that the cat was just showing off.[11] I looked up in time to see it fall. It crawled up, then fell again.

We talked for an hour and had apple pie and coffee, slowly. Finally, we got up with Carolyn taking my hand. Slightly embarrassed, I tried to pull away but her grip held me. I let her have her way[12] as she led me down the hallway with her mother right behind me. When I opened the door, I was startled[13] by a kitten clinging to the screen door, its mouth screaming "cat food, dog biscuits, *sushi*... ." I opened the door and the kitten, still holding on, whined in the language of hungry animals. When I got into Carolyn's car, I looked back: the cat was still clinging. I asked Carolyn if it were possibly hungry, but she said the cat was being silly. She started the car, waved to her mother, and bounced us over the rain-poked drive, patting my thigh for being her lover baby. Carolyn waved again. I looked back, waving, then gawking at a window screen where there were now three kittens clawing and screaming to get in. Like Mexicans, I thought. I remembered the Molinas and how the cats clung to their screens—cats they shot down with squirt guns. On the highway, I felt happy, pleased by it all. I patted Carolyn's thigh. Her people were like Mexicans, only different.

12

13

---

11 **showing off**   trying to get attention
12 **have her way**   do what she wants
13 **startled**   surprised

ABOUT THE AUTHOR
Gary Soto is the author of eight volumes of poetry and nine volumes of prose. He currently teaches at the University of California at Berkeley.

5. On your own. The sentences below are from the short story. Use context to guess the meaning of the <u>underlined</u> words in each sentence. Then look up each word in a dictionary and choose the definition that best fits the meaning of the word in this context.

READING STRATEGY:
Using Context
See page 255.

a. "She [My grandmother] saved the calendar away and we went to the living room where she lectured me on the <u>virtues</u> of the Mexican girl: first, she could cook and, second, she acted like a woman, not a man, in her husband's home."

My guess: _____

Dictionary definition: _____

b. "When I asked about Jews, whom I had read about, she asked for a picture. I rode home on my bicycle and returned with a calendar <u>depicting</u> the important races of the world."

My guess: _____

Dictionary definition: _____

c. "Steam curled from a pot of boiling beans, the radio was on, looking as <u>squat</u> as a loaf of bread."

My guess: _____

Dictionary definition: _____

d. "I called him [my friend Scott] and his mother pointed to the side of the house where his bedroom was a small aluminum trailer, the kind you <u>gawk</u> at when they're flipped over on the freeway, wheels spinning in the air."

My guess: _____

Dictionary definition: _____

e. "He had his girl and I had mine. But our seventh-grade vision was the same: to marry, get jobs, buy cars and maybe a house if we had money <u>left over</u>."

My guess: _____

Dictionary definition: _____

f. "We bought a bag of popcorn at Penneys and sat on a bench near the fountain watching Mexican and Okie girls pass. 'That one's mine,' I pointed with my chin when a girl with eyebrows arched into black rainbows <u>ambled</u> by."

My guess: _____

Dictionary definition: _____

g. "I was in love and there was <u>no looking back</u>. She was the one."

My guess: _____

Dictionary definition: _____

h. "When we pulled into the drive, I panicked and begged Carolyn to <u>make a U-turn</u> and go back so we could talk about it over a soda."

My guess: _____

Dictionary definition: _____

WRITING STRATEGY:
Providing Details
See page 246.

6. **On your own.** Do you agree or disagree with the statements below? Circle your answer. Then find information in the story to support your opinion.

a. The narrator didn't like Okies.   AGREE   (DISAGREE)

   His best friend Scott was an Okie. _____

b. The narrator's family was rich.   AGREE   DISAGREE

_____

c. Carolyn's family was rich.   AGREE   DISAGREE

_____

d. Carolyn's mother couldn't speak English.   AGREE   DISAGREE

_____

e. The narrator wanted Carolyn's parents to like him.

AGREE   DISAGREE

_____

Share ideas with your classmates.

7. **Pair Work.** Choose a scene in the story in which two characters interact. Rewrite this scene in dialogue form and then practice reading your lines, using appropriate body language. After practicing several times, describe the setting to your classmates and act out the scene.

8. **On your own.** Reread the part of the story in which the narrator visits Carolyn's family. What details does the writer provide to help you picture Carolyn's home? List them in the chart below.

WRITING STRATEGY:
Providing Details
See page 246.

Sights	Sounds	Smells
cracked window		

9. **On your own.** Using your chart from Activity 8, write a description of Carolyn's home. Pretend that you are there, visiting Carolyn's family. Use the details in your chart to answer these questions:

   a. What do you see?

   b. What do you hear?

   c. What can you smell?

   After you finish writing, read your description to a classmate.

READING STRATEGY:
Asking Questions
See page 249.

10. **Group Work.** Follow the steps below to share ideas about the story.

    a. Work together to write a list of questions about the story. Ask questions that really interest you.

    Examples:

    > *Are all Mexican women like the ones that the grandmother describes in the first paragraph?*

    > *In the fourth paragraph, why does Scott say that he would never marry a Mexican? Why does he feel this way?*

    b. From your list choose the three questions that interest you most and write them on another piece of paper.

    c. Exchange questions with another group.

    d. Discuss the other group's questions and take notes on your answers.

    e. Get together with the other group and report your answers to their questions. Listen carefully to their answers to your questions and take notes.

    f. Read your questions aloud to the class and report the other group's answers.

11. **On your own.** Based on the information in the article "The Secrets of Marital Bliss," do you think the narrator of the short story and his wife will "stick together for the long haul?" Why or why not? Explore these questions as you write in your journal.

CRITICAL THINKING STRATEGY:
Synthesizing
See page 263.

12. **Writing Project.** Do you think it is important to marry someone from the same cultural background? From the same social class? In writing, present your ideas. Here are some suggestions to help you get started:

   a. Quickwrite for five minutes, taking the position that it *is* important to marry someone from the same cultural background. Then write for several minutes, taking the position that it is *not* necessary to marry someone from the same cultural background. Look over your quickwriting and decide which position you will take in your writing.

WRITING STRATEGY:
Quickwriting
See page 246.

   b. In your journal, state your answer to the question, *Do you think it is important to marry someone from the same cultural background?* Then list your reasons. For each reason, think of details and examples to illustrate your ideas.

WRITING STRATEGY:
Providing Details
See page 246.

Understanding Your Audience
See page 247.

   c. Think about who your audience will be. A friend who is thinking about getting married? Your classmates and teacher? The readers of your school newspaper? Note your thoughts below.

   Probable audience:

   _____

   d. Consider what your audience knows about the topic and what they might be interested in reading about. Keep these thoughts in mind as you write a first draft of your paper.

   e. Place a copy of your paper in your writing folder.

You now have four pieces of writing from Unit 5, one from the writing assignment at the end of each chapter. Each piece of writing is a rough draft— a collection of first ideas.

Your final project is to revise one of these first drafts. You will probably want to choose the one that interests you most.

There is no formula for revising and no simple steps to follow. For many writers, though, revising involves the following:

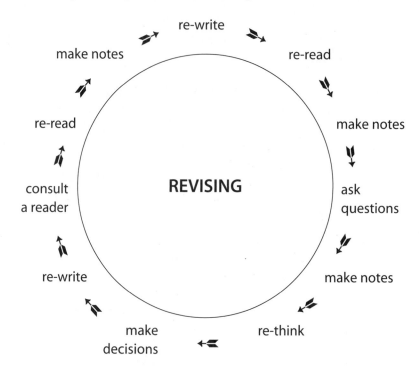

You might repeat any part of the process a number of times before you are satisfied with a piece of writing.

As you revise your writing for Unit Five, you, your classmates, and your teacher may want to use the checklist to help you evaluate your drafts. Write and rewrite until you can check off everything on the list.

Unit Five
Revising Checklist

Yes ✓

Sharpening your focus	First draft	Second draft	Third draft	Final draft
• Is it clear who the audience is?	❑	❑	❑	❑
• Is the topic limited enough?	❑	❑	❑	❑
• Have unnecessary words been deleted?	❑	❑	❑	❑
Making your writing interesting				
• Does the introduction "hook" the reader?	❑	❑	❑	❑
• Does the writer use interesting details?	❑	❑	❑	❑
• Does the writer's voice come through?	❑	❑	❑	❑
Helping your reader follow your ideas				
• Does the title suggest the writer's thinking?	❑	❑	❑	❑
• Does the introduction guide the reader?	❑	❑	❑	❑
• Can the reader perceive the writer's plan?	❑	❑	❑	❑
Polishing your ideas				
• Do the sentences vary in length?	❑	❑	❑	❑
• Are the ideas connected?	❑	❑	❑	❑
• Are the verb forms and tenses correct?	❑	❑	❑	❑
• Are the punctuation and spelling correct?	❑	❑	❑	❑

Your final draft may be placed in a class booklet, along with your classmates' writing. You can pass the booklet around for everyone to read.

235

Reference Guide

Writing Strategies

001 BRAINSTORMING

Brainstorming is a good way to collect ideas for writing. It is an especially useful strategy to use with a partner or with a group of people.

Follow these steps to brainstorm a set of ideas:

- Put your writing idea on a piece of paper. This might be a word, a phrase, or a question.
- Write down every idea that this writing idea brings to mind. Don't evaluate your ideas. Just think and write quickly. If you are brainstorming in a group, you may want to have one member of the group write down ideas as everyone contributes orally.

Example:

Writing idea: Growing old

thinning hair

time to enjoy family

fun with grandchildren

aches and pains

less work

reflect on what's really important

After brainstorming, reread your list and circle the ideas you might want to use in your writing.

002 CITING SOURCES

In school writing, you are expected to use others' ideas to introduce and/or support something you want to say. Ideas may come from something you've heard or read. In any case, you need to note where the ideas come from.

Here are some ways to credit your source of ideas:

- Leon Lederman, a Nobel Prize-winning scientist, credits dedication and imagination for his success (*Christian Science Monitor*). Lederman is not the only... .

- "We want to keep our environment pure and clean," says Edward Cornish, president of World Future Society, a group that studies socio-logical and technological trends. Jobs in environmental preservation will be in demand, according to Cornish.

- According to Judson Landis, a sociologist, parents act differently towards their children based on their gender.

- In the short story "Who's Hu?," a young Chinese immigrant discovers that American girls aren't supposed to be good in math. This is only one kind of gender stereotyping that exists in American society... .

Others' ideas help you explain your ideas to your readers. Citing sources also gives your writing an air of authority. You are an "expert" because you share ideas with experts.

003 COLLECTING INFORMATION

Before you start writing, spend plenty of time collecting ideas and information. This will make your writing task much easier.

Here are a few suggestions for collecting information:

- Quickwrite about your topic for several minutes. Then look over your quickwriting for good ideas to use in your writing. (See 013 Quickwriting.)

- Write your topic on a piece of paper and then list every idea that comes to mind. Look back over your list and choose ideas to develop. (See 007 Listing Ideas.)

- Think about your topic and write your ideas on a cluster diagram. (See 008 Making a Cluster Diagram.)

- If your topic is in two parts (two cities, two people, etc.) and you want to look at sameness and difference, write your ideas on a Venn diagram. (See 010 Making a Venn diagram.)

- Look up your topic in the library and find other articles to read about your topic. Take notes. Be sure to write down the title, author, publisher, and page numbers of the articles you take notes from. (You must always credit the source of your information; see 002, Citing Sources.)

- Interview one or more people to get their ideas on the topic.

004 FINDING A TOPIC

In some school courses, you will have to find your own writing topic. Your teacher may give you general guidelines: for example, "a 2–3 page paper analyzing some aspect of gender stereotyping."

Before you panic, think about these "rules" for finding a topic:

- Focus on a <u>limited</u> topic. The shorter the paper, the more limited the topic. "The psychological effects of gender stereotyping" is too broad a topic for a 2–3 page paper.

- Choose a topic on which you can find specific information.

- Look through your textbook, journal, and other class assignments for topic ideas. Fill up a page with ideas that interest you. When the page is full, go back and circle the ones you want to "keep." From the circled ideas, choose one and quickwrite about it for five to ten minutes. If your quickwriting goes "nowhere," choose another one and quickwrite again. Repeat the process until you find one that might work.

- Give yourself a few days to decide. Carry a notebook with you and jot down ideas as they come to you; check the library for information on the topic(s) you are considering; discuss possibilities with a classmate and your teacher. Take notes as you think, talk, and listen.

- Expect to put time and energy into choosing a topic. The night before the paper is due is <u>not</u> a good time to find a topic.

005 FOCUSING YOUR IDEAS

Think of yourself as a photographer: you may know what you want to photograph, but you also have to consider distance and angle. From far away, details are lost; too close, and the setting disappears. A wrong angle can chop off someone's head. Focusing your writing for your readers is like focusing a camera.

Compare the following:

Unfocused writing

Martin Luther King received worldwide acclaim for his civil rights work when he was awarded the Nobel Peace Prize. Joseph Webre, a Benedictine monk, bakes hundreds of loaves of bread to give to the poor in his New Orleans community. Wangari Maathai, founder of the Green Belt movement, began her tree-planting project in her own backyard. Famous and not-so-famous people have worked for social change... .

Focused writing

By 3:30 every morning, Father Joseph Webre is working in the bakery of St. Joseph Abbey to bake hundreds of loaves of bread he will later distribute to the poor of New Orleans. Unknown, except by those who receive his gift of hope and love, Father Joe is one of many activists working for social change in their own communities... .

Here are some guidelines for focusing your writing:

- Limit the scope of your topic. The shorter the paper, the more narrow the focus.
- Quickwrite about your topic to "test" the focus. If your quickwriting moves your thinking into details, your focus is probably narrow enough. (See 013 Quickwriting; see also 011 Organizing Ideas.)
- Think about your readers. Tell them what you think they don't already know. Resist the urge to tell them everything you know.
- Build details, examples, and quotations into your writing. Readers want to "see" and "hear" what you mean. (See 006 Giving Examples, 012 Providing Details, and 016 Using Quotations.)

006 GIVING EXAMPLES

Giving examples helps your reader to understand your ideas. It is also a good way to convince your reader that what you say is true.

Example:

My grandmother is such an active person that it is hard to believe she is 93 years old. She still drives her old Chevy, though she now stays off the California freeways and keeps close to home. She reads voraciously— magazines, books, and newspapers.

Main Idea: *My grandmother is very active.*

Examples: *She still drives a car.*

She reads a lot.

007 LISTING IDEAS

Making a list is a good strategy for collecting ideas. Simply write your topic on a piece of paper. Then think about your topic and write down any important or useful ideas that come to mind. You can go back later and choose your best ideas.

Example:

Topic: *reasons for moving to Toronto*
- *needed a job*
- *had friends there*
- *wanted to live in a big city*
- *wanted to be near my sister*

008 MAKING A CLUSTER DIAGRAM

Making a cluster diagram is a good way to collect ideas before you start writing. Making a cluster diagram can also help you see connections between big ideas and details.

Follow these steps to make a cluster diagram:

1. Write your topic in the center of a piece of paper. Circle it.

2. Think about your topic. What words and ideas come to mind? Write each thought in a smaller circle and connect it by a line to the circle in the center.

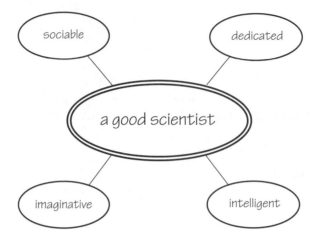

3. Think about the ideas in the smaller circles. Write down any ideas that come to mind and connect them to the smaller circles. (See the diagram on the following page.)

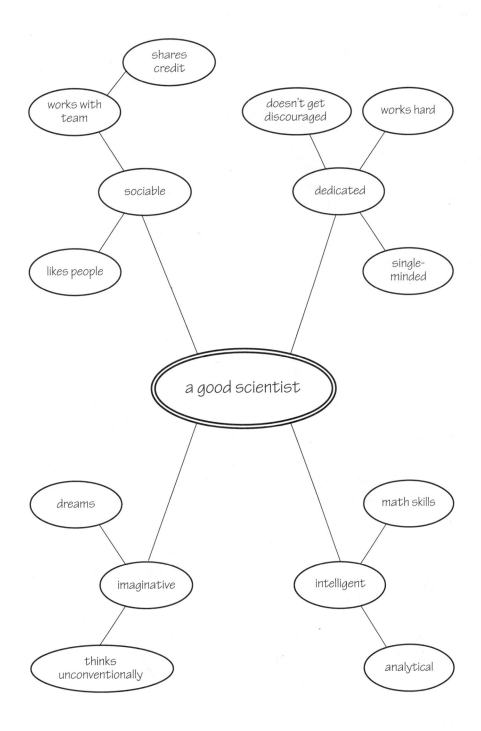

009 MAKING A TREE DIAGRAM

Making a tree diagram is a useful way to organize your ideas before you start writing. Before you make a tree diagram, you might want to first list ideas about your topic. Then reread your list of ideas looking for categories of information. Write these categories on your tree diagram. Then list ideas in each category.

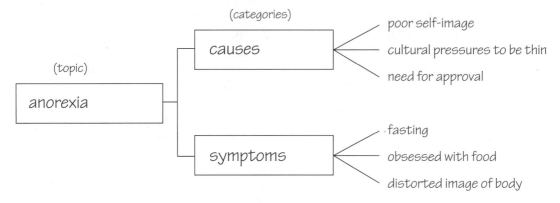

010 MAKING A VENN DIAGRAM

If you want to compare and contrast two things, you can use a Venn diagram to collect ideas. In the center of the diagram (where the circles overlap) list ways the two things are alike. In the outer circles, list ways they are different.

On the Venn diagram below, one writer compares and contrasts two social activists—Martin Luther King and Mohandas Gandhi.

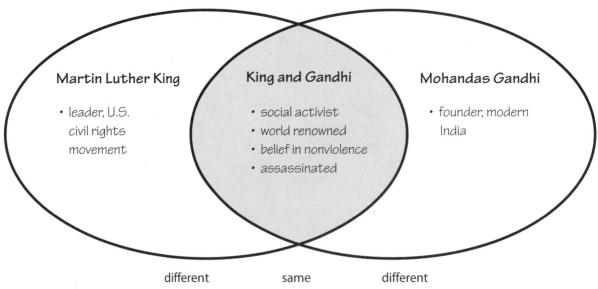

011 ORGANIZING IDEAS

Some writers prefer to organize their ideas before they start writing. Others prefer to get started by quickwriting and organize their ideas later. (See 013 Quickwriting.)

If you like to organize before you start writing, here are some strategies to use:

❖ **Taking notes in a chart is a good way to collect and organize ideas for writing.** To make a chart, think about the kinds of information you want to organize. List this information as headings in your chart. Then add ideas and examples under each heading.

Example: *writing about growth areas in the U.S. job market*

Field of Work	Jobs Available	Reasons for Growth
health care	*nurses*	*population growing older*
education	*teachers*	*children of baby boomers reaching school age*
financial services	*accountants*	*more reliance on information*

❖ **Making an outline is a good way to organize your ideas.** Keep in mind, however, that your outline is only a plan. You can change your ideas at any time.

Example:

    I. Introduction: Family traditions are important to a child's security.

        • Traditions give a child a sense of belonging.

        • Traditions give a child an identity.

    II. Reasons why family traditions give a child a sense of belonging

        • Tell about my own family traditions.

        • Cite Amy Tan or Maxine Hong Kingston.

    III. Reasons why traditions help a child establish an identity

        • Cite efforts to revive Cherokee language: "can't separate language and culture."

    IV. Conclusion

❖ **A very good way to organize your ideas is to write a thesis sentence.** A thesis sentence is really an organizing tool. It expresses your organizing idea for writing.

> ***Example:*** *Family traditions help a child establish an identity and a sense of belonging.*

❖ **Choose a "working" title.** Sometimes a title will help you organize and focus your ideas. You can change the title later, if you think of a better one.

012 PROVIDING DETAILS

Details in your writing help to keep your reader's attention. They also help your reader understand your ideas. From vivid words, the reader should be able to see, hear, smell, and feel what you are describing. From examples, the reader can understand what you are explaining. The rule of thumb is this: *Show, don't tell.*

Here are some ways to provide details in your writing:

Example:

• Use specific nouns.

General	Specific
car	*a Toyota*
a drink	*lemonade*
dessert	*apple pie*

• Use specific verbs.

General	Specific
look	*stare*
talk	*discuss*
walk	*stroll*

• Use "concrete" words.

Abstract	Concrete
Marie seemed excited.	*She jumped up and down, clapping her hands and grinning from ear to ear.*

013 QUICKWRITING

Quickwriting is a useful way to collect ideas for writing.

Follow these steps to quickwrite:

1. Choose a topic—something you want to write about.

2. For five to ten minutes, write quickly. Don't worry about grammar or spelling. If you can't think of a word in English, write it in your native language. The important thing is to write without stopping.

3. If you can't think of anything to write, put that down or write the same word over and over again.

4. When you have finished writing, read over your ideas. Circle the ideas that you like best.

Example:

Writing topic: Growing old

I'm not really looking forward to growing old. Is anyone? I think about my grandmother and how difficult her life is. She's 93 now. Many of her friends are dead. She can't do a lot of things now. She has trouble walking, and she can't hear very well. But she says that inside she feels very young.... I can't think of anything to write. My grandmother's body is getting old, but her mind is young. She reads all of the time and she still likes to try new things. She's learning to paint... .

014 UNDERSTANDING YOUR AUDIENCE

Your readers are your audience—your classmates, a friend, your teacher, or someone you don't even know. Before you start writing, it is important to have a clear idea of who your readers are. What you say in your writing will depend in part on who your audience is.

Keep these questions in mind while you write:

• Who is going to read this piece of writing?

• What do my readers already know about the topic?

• Is the readers' background different from mine? If so, how?

• What will interest my readers?

• What questions will my readers have?

015 USING POINT OF VIEW

Before you write, you need to decide how you are going to "see" your topic. For example, are you going to look at your topic through the eyes of a student? A friend? A parent? A professional? Someone else?

How you see your topic **is** your point of view.

Example:

In "Why I Quit the Company," Tomoyuki Iwashita writes as an unhappy employee:

> …*My life rapidly became reduced to a shuttle between the dorm and the office. The working day is officially eight hours, but you can never leave the office on time. I used to work from nine in the morning until eight or nine at night, and often until midnight.*

In *The Hopeland*, K. Kam writes as an adult, looking back at her parents' lives with regret and frustration.

> …*Their words seep into my blood and cause my muscles to pull taut.*

In "Learning Gender Roles," Judson Landis "speaks" as a professional sociologist.

> …*The results of gender-role stereotyping are many and varied.*

Your point of view *shapes* your writing. How a writer "speaks" as a child is different from how a writer "speaks" as a teenager or a professional person. As a writer, you can write from many different points of view.

016 USING QUOTATIONS

As a writer, you'll want to build the words and ideas of other people into your writing. This gives it authority. After all, you are an "expert" if you find experts who think like you.

In school writing, you are expected to work "across texts." This means that your readers expect you to use ideas and information from other texts (essays, articles, stories, etc.) to develop and support your ideas.

Sometimes you build in the words and ideas of other writers with a direct quotation:

Example:

"The traditions I grew up with gave me a security greater than money could ever buy," says Tencha Avila, a writer who grew up in a Mexican-American family. I too was given traditions more valuable than money. From my Moroccan grandparents, I learned… .

Sometimes you weave others' words and ideas into your writing more indirectly:

Example:

According to John Tepper Marlin, author of "The Best Places in the U.S.," the best place to make money is New York City. My experience in New York City tells me otherwise. For me, New York City was a complete financial disaster….

Reading Strategies

017 ASKING QUESTIONS

Asking yourself questions is a useful strategy to use before you read, while you read, and after you finish reading. It can help you understand and remember.

Before you read, study the title and any headings or pictures and then ask questions such as these:

- What is the article about?
- What do I already know about the topic?
- What do I want to find out about the topic?

While you are reading, stop frequently to ask yourself questions:

- What is this paragraph about?
- What is the writer saying here?
- What is my reaction to this idea?

After you finish reading, ask questions about what you've read:

- What was the subject? What was the main idea?
- What was interesting to me? What did I learn?
- How do any of these ideas connect to my own experience? To other texts?

018 DISTINGUISHING FACT AND OPINION

A *fact* is something that is objectively true; it is real. An *opinion,* on the other hand, is what a person believes or concludes; an opinion has no proof.

Writers give facts in their writing; they also express opinions. When you read, you need to distinguish between the two.

Example:

Fact	Opinion
Mohandas Gandhi was born in	*Gandhi is revered by Indians*
India in 1869.	*as the founder of their nation.*

Writers don't need to support their facts; a fact is simply true. However, writers do need to explain and support their opinions. Supporting details can convince a reader that a writer's opinions are sound.

019 FINDING MAIN IDEAS

Main ideas are the key points around which a writer organizes a piece of writing. A good writer includes a lot of supporting details, but limits the key ideas to one or two. Here's some help to find main ideas:

❖ Sometimes organizing ideas are stated directly. In your own book, you might underline important ideas that help you follow the writer's thinking.

Example:

> *Most career counselors tell their clients that the key to job satisfaction is finding a line of work they are interested in and enjoy. But <u>for those about to embark on a course of training or study…there is comfort in knowing there will be a demand for their skills</u> down the road.*
> *So we look to the U.S. Bureau of Labor Statistics for projections on the occupations that will be most in demand over the next decade. Health care dominates… .*

❖ Sometimes a writer does not state key ideas directly. Instead, you must infer them as you read. (See 023 Making Inferences.)

Here are some strategies to help you infer main ideas:

• Study details and examples.

• Look for ways the ideas are related. Ask yourself what they have in common.

• Think of a general claim that can be supported by the details.

Example:

> *In 1948, only three years after arriving in the United States from China, An Wang earned a Ph.D. in Physics from Harvard University. After receiving his degree, he stayed at Harvard and worked in the Computation*

Laboratory. It was at this time that he invented the magnetic core. This device was a basic part of computer memory.

In 1951 Wang decided that he was tired of working for others. With a savings of $600, he started his own company, Wang Laboratories....

Your claim, supported by the details:

In his first years in the United States, Wang accomplished a great deal.

❖ As you read, look for a writer's main ideas next to specific details in a text. Main ideas are more general; they provide an "umbrella" for details.

Take the short text about jobs above. When you get to details ("occupations most in demand: health care," etc.), you know the writer is supporting a general point. If you missed it, back up and see what is going on.

020 MAKING A STORY OUTLINE

Making a story outline helps you to focus on important information in a story. When you make a story outline, look for these main parts of a story:

Characters:	*Who are the people in the story?*
Setting:	*Where and when does the story take place?*
The problem:	*What is the central issue? What are the characters trying to do?*
Important events:	*What happens in the story?*

021 MAKING A TIME LINE

Making a time line is a way to organize information visually. It helps you see the order of events over time. It can also help you find examples of cause and effect.

A time line helps you keep track of what you read; you can take notes in a time line.

Example:

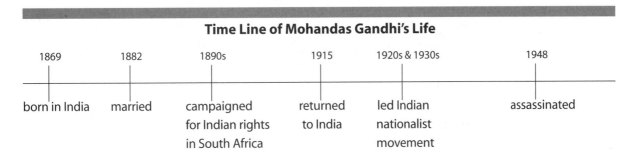

Time Line of Mohandas Gandhi's Life

1869	1882	1890s	1915	1920s & 1930s	1948
born in India	married	campaigned for Indian rights in South Africa	returned to India	led Indian nationalist movement	assassinated

022 MAKING A TREE DIAGRAM

Making a tree diagram is a useful way to organize ideas when you read. Here are some suggestions for making the diagram:

- List the topic of your reading to the left.
- Look for categories of information the writer uses to develop the topic. Write them on your diagram.
- List supporting information to the right of each category.

Example: *You read an article on anorexia, an eating disorder.*

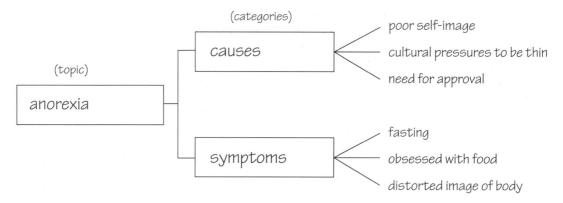

023 MAKING INFERENCES

An inference is a reasonable conclusion based on evidence.

Example:

Evidence: *Your friend has a broken leg.*

Inference: *Your friend had an accident.*

Writers often use details to suggest their general claim rather than stating it directly. Readers must then infer, or guess, the claim from the writer's supporting details.

Example:

Supporting Evidence: *Dr. An Wang, who immigrated from China as a poor student and later founded a very successful computer company, gave a lot of money during his lifetime to support programs for the arts, education, and medical research.*

Inference: *Dr. Wang was a very generous man.*

024 PARAPHRASING

Paraphrasing means putting ideas into your own words. If you paraphrase while you read, you can check your understanding as you go along.

Paraphrasing when you finish reading is a good way to check your comprehension. If you can't paraphrase what you have read, you need to read it again.

Paraphrasing can also help you remember what you've read. You can use your paraphrases as notes, if you want to review for a test. You can also refer to your notes later when you write.

Example:

Text: *"Like other roles, gender roles are learned through the socialization process. It is possible that in our society the teaching of gender roles starts even earlier than the teaching of other roles."*

Your Paraphrase: *Starting almost from birth, males learn what it means to be "a boy" in their culture, and females learn what it means to be "a girl."*

025 PREDICTING

What is the weather going to be like tomorrow? What is the next paragraph in this reading going to be about? What is going to happen to the main character in this story? When you answer these questions, you are predicting.

When you predict, you use what you already know (your "crystal ball") to make a logical prediction.

Example:

The title of the fable I am going to read is "The Dog and the Wolf." I already know that a fable is a narrative that teaches a lesson. I know that the characters in a fable are often animals that speak and act like human beings. Let's see…a dog is a domestic animal and a wolf is a wild animal. Maybe the fable is about being free. The wolf is free, while the dog is not.

Predictions help you focus on what you're reading. You make a prediction and then you read to check if it's accurate.

026 PREVIEWING

The word *preview* means "to look before." To preview what you're going to read, look it over before you start reading. Here are some suggestions.

- Look at the title and ask yourself questions about it. Then predict answers to your questions.

- Look at the pictures and predict what the reading is about.
- Recall what you already know about the topic.
- Read the first paragraph and the last paragraph and try to figure out the main idea of the reading.
- Set a purpose for reading. Decide what you hope to find out as you read.

027 READING FOR SPECIFIC INFORMATION

Sometimes your purpose for reading is limited. You don't want to know everything; you only want answers to specific questions.

Example:

> You are reading an article on the expansion of the Sahara Desert. Maybe you only want to know how fast the Sahara is expanding. Then, as you read, you look for numbers and periods of time, such as "two kilometers per year" or "one acre a month."

If you know what you are looking for, then you can focus on the limited possibilities. You can read quickly by scanning for this information. (See 028 Scanning.)

028 SCANNING

Scanning means looking quickly for specific information. Here are some suggestions:

- Let your eyes move quickly down the page. Don't read every word.
- Slow down when you see words or phrases that might be important to you.
- Check (✓) or underline words or phrases that you think are important.

Scanning saves time if you are collecting ideas or specific pieces of information.

029 SUMMARIZING

When you summarize, you restate ideas and information briefly in your own words. Here are some suggestions for writing a summary:

- Begin with a reference to the author and/or title of the article. Include also the source (book, newspaper, etc.) of the article.
- Include only the writer's main ideas and key points.
- Condense everything into a short paragraph. If your summary is longer, you are probably including unnecessary details.

Sample Summary:

According to Judson Landis, in "Learning Gender Roles," gender roles are learned through the socialization process. Landis claims that the process begins early in the home and is reinforced at school. Results of gender-stereotyping are numerous and varied, Landis says, and not all of the benefits are for males. (See full text on pages 48–49.)

Writing a summary of what you've read helps you check your understanding of the reading. If you can summarize it, you know you understand it.

Writing a summary also helps you remember the main points of what you've read. You can also read over your summary later to review for a test or to find ideas to use in your next piece of writing.

Teachers may ask you to write summaries as "proof" that you've completed their reading assignments. In some classes, you may also need to write summaries of work (a research paper, etc.) that you *plan* to do. This "promissory" summary needs to include your topic, the key points you plan to make, and the source(s) of your information. If a teacher assigns this kind of summary, or abstract, ask for a model that can guide you in writing your own.

030 TAKING NOTES IN A CHART

Taking notes as you read helps you organize and remember important information. When you take notes, write down the most important information. Here is one type of chart you might use:

Main ideas	Details
effects of gender-role stereotyping	• *males restrict their emotions*
	• *males feel more pressure to achieve*
	• *males' stress probably contributes to shorter life expectancy, more heart disease, higher suicide rates, more mental illness*
	• *fewer career choices for males/females*
	• *females get less help at school*

031 USING CONTEXT

Sometimes you can figure out the meaning of a difficult word by looking at the context—the other words in the sentence or nearby sentences. Like a detective, you have to look for clues.

Here are some context clues to look for:

A definition:

*It was at this time that An Wang invented the **magnetic core**. <u>This device was a basic part of computer memory</u> until the use of microchips in the late 1960s.*

A description:

*The old woman's two sons were **peddlers**. <u>The older one sold umbrellas and the younger sold straw shoes.</u>*

A comparison or contrast:

*My nephew <u>loved</u> the first story, <u>but</u> he **despised** the second one.*

A series:

*<u>Pizza,</u> **submarines,** and <u>hamburgers</u> are popular in the United States, especially among young people.*

Cause and effect:

*This house makes me **miserable** <u>because it is dark and gloomy.</u>*

Setting:

*After a late dinner, the man put a sack of rice on his back and **set out for** his <u>brother's house. There was a full moon and he could see the path clearly</u>.*

Example:

*Jacob Blitzstein is warm and **gregarious**. <u>He likes to hear a good joke, enjoys the company of others, and loves to tell a good story.</u>*

Synonym:

*According to his lawyer, Abraham Lincoln was the most **reticent**—<u>secretive</u>—man that ever lived.*

Combinations of clues:

*Want to <u>start a business?</u> Central cities always have been hospitable to **entrepreneurs,** because these areas provide easy access to <u>buyers and producers.</u>*

032 WRITING MARGIN NOTES

Writing notes in the margin of your books helps you to read actively.

Here are some types of notes you might write in the margin:

- Consciously react to the text—*"Great idea!" "I'm glad that's not me!" "I feel sorry for her!" "Hmmm, I don't think that's such a great idea!"* Etc.

- Write down questions as you read: *"Why are they doing that?" "What will happen next?" "What will the results be?" "What is the main idea here?"* Etc.

- Connect your own knowledge and experience to the text: *"The same think happened to me!" "My parents didn't think this way." "No, it was different for me."* Etc.

- Connect ideas from other texts you have read: *"Just like in 'Who's Hu?'— American girls aren't supposed to be good in math. Landis would agree: gender roles are learned through socialization process. Process differs from culture to culture."*

Here is an example showing how margin notes might look:

Example:

(your notes)	(text)
I remember a place like this in Toronto.	*…If you sat upstairs, near the oval-shaped windows, you could watch the street scene, which in Chicago neighborhoods is always interesting— women in furs alongside men rummaging through garbage cans. The Bagel Nosh was a microcosm of the neighborhood.*
Reminder: Look up "microcosm." Like my kitchen table! Put book under leg.	*The Bagel Nosh was nothing fancy. The tables often needed a matchbook to balance their legs. To find a spot, you sometimes had to clear the table of dirty dishes from a previous customer. You couldn't rave about the food either—warmed-over potato pancakes, apple strudel, lox, cheese blintzes—the usual deli fare.…*
Wonder what kind of food this is—I've never tasted it.	

Critical Thinking Strategies

033 ANALYZING

When you analyze something, you examine it. You put it under a microscope, so to speak. You study it from every angle to see what it is, how it works, and how everything fits together.

When you analyze what you hear or read, you probably want to know causes, effects, reasons, purposes, or consequences. To analyze, you need to ask questions: *what, why, when, who, how,* and *how much/many.*

Example:

You hear about a multi-car crash on the interstate. Questions of analysis immediately come to mind:

- *How many cars were involved?*
- *Was anyone killed? How many people were injured?*
- *What caused the pile-up? Fog? Smoke? Rain? Was speed a factor?*
- *What time of day (or night) did the accident occur?*

If you ask the right questions and get informative answers, you get the full picture.

Your teachers will expect you to analyze what you read. To analyze a text (article, essay, short story, etc.), here are some questions to ask yourself:

- *What/who is this text about?*
- *What is the context? What are the circumstances?*
- *What is the central issue or problem?*
- *What questions does the writer ask?*
- *What questions does the writer answer?*
- *What is the writer's central point(s)?*
- *So what? What does it all mean?*
- *How can I connect this text to other texts that I have read?*
- *How can I apply this to what I know?*

When you write, your readers need to be able to answer the same questions.

034 APPLYING WHAT YOU KNOW

Applying what you know means taking ideas from one context and using them to understand or change another context.

You can apply what you learn from reading to your life, or from your life to your reading:

Example:

You read this:
Medical studies show that sick people get well faster if they feel cared for and loved.

You apply the idea to your own life:
You think about your sick uncle. You haven't telephoned or visited him lately. Based on what you have read, you decide to visit him more often and telephone him every day. Maybe your attention will contribute to his recovery.

In school, you also need to apply what you learn from one text to another text:

Example:

You read a text by sociologist Judson Landis:
"Like other roles, gender roles are learned through the socialization process.... [In Western culture,] the male is restricted in how he may show emotion: He is strong and silent, he does not show weakness, and he keeps his feelings under careful rein, at least outwardly...."

Then you read a text by Samir Khalaf, a concerned parent:
"I could see him fret as [Lebanese] relatives and friends he has not seen for two years try, in vain, to solicit a hug or a kiss on the forehead. The reluctant denial has been transformed into a boast, that he is now an "American boy.""

You apply what you know from one text to the other, something like this:
Khalaf's experience with his son, George, is a perfect example of what Landis is talking about. As George becomes socialized into the new culture, he is more reluctant to show emotion. He must think that he has to keep his feelings under "careful rein," as Landis says, in order to be an "American boy." It's sad that he is losing the spontaneous expression of emotion of his family's culture.

As you read and write, you need to make these connections and apply what you know.

035 CLASSIFYING

Classifying means arranging and organizing into groups, classes, or categories. For example, we classify when we separate *good* from *bad, general* from *specific, cause* from *effect.*

To classify, you need to find general ideas that allow you to "cluster" the details:

Example:

(unclassified information)
brown eyes, curious, intelligent, beautiful smile, likes people, tall and thin, dark hair, easy to please

(classified information)

Physical traits	**Personality traits**
brown eyes	*curious*
beautiful smile	*intelligent*
tall and thin	*likes people*
dark hair	*easy to please*

When you cluster ideas, your reader can follow your writing easily. When you recognize another writer's categories, you read with better understanding.

036 COMPARING

Comparing is one way to analyze a topic: you look for similarities and/or differences. How are ideas, places, people, and situations the **same?** How are they **different?**

As a writer, you might compare by arranging ideas "side by side":

> *For years, America was called a "melting pot," a place where the customs of many people melted or blended into one American culture.* *Today, however, some call the country a "salad bowl," a society made up of different peoples and cultures who are "mixed" together, yet remain separate.*

Writers often need special language for comparing:

> *Researchers <u>agree that</u> the most critical task of a marriage is to create a style of communication that honors both partners' need for love and respect.*

> *Researchers find that men in general are <u>much more</u> uncomfortable with conflict in relationships and thus <u>more likely</u> to withdraw from a potential argument.*

> *According to Avshalom Caspi, a psychologist, the secret to happiness in marriage is to marry someone like yourself, <u>while</u> John Gottman, a professor of psychology, believes it is the ability to handle differences, <u>not</u> similarity, that helps spouses stay together.*

When you read, notice the language and arrangement of ideas. When you realize a writer is comparing, look for similarities and/or differences.

As a reader or writer, it helps to visualize similarities and differences in a Venn diagram (010 Making a Venn Diagram) or a chart (030 Taking Notes in a Chart).

037 EVALUATING

To evaluate, you make a judgment. *Good or bad? Better or worse? More important or less important? True or untrue?* We evaluate when we answer these questions.

Your evaluation is your opinion. There are no right or wrong answers to questions of opinion. Whenever you evaluate, however, your readers/listeners expect you to <u>explain</u> your logic and <u>support</u> your claim.

Example:

> *You judge honesty to be important in a marriage.*

> **(You explain your logic.)**

> • *A solid relationship needs to be built on trust.*

> • *To be trustworthy, a spouse has to be honest.*

> • *If a spouse cheats or lies, the relationship suffers.*

> **(You might illustrate from your experience.)**

> *I once knew a young couple. In fact, they were my close friends. They promised to trust each other and always tell each other the truth. One day, the wife discovered that her husband had been cheating on her from the very beginning of their marriage. He had had numerous affairs with other women, while she had been completely faithful to him. Needless to say, she was devastated. Her trust in her husband was broken, and the couple subsequently divorced.*

038 INTERPRETING

As you read, *your* ideas and feelings are just as important to your understanding as whatever the writer intends to say. This means that two readers can understand the same sentence or whole text in two different ways—and both can be right!

When you interpret something, you talk about its meaning or significance to you. You might answer some of these questions:

- What does _____ X _____ mean?
- What does _____ X _____ mean to me?
- What experience(s) in my life help(s) me understand this?
- How do I see it?

Explain your ideas when you interpret. To support your interpretation, give reasons, facts, and details from the text, from another text, or from your own experience:

Example:

> Sandra Cisneros, a Mexican-American writer, says that "people's cultures are what make them special." To me, this means that a people's language and customs give them a unique means of identifying themselves and identifying with each other.
>
> It's sometimes easier for someone outside a culture to define that "specialness." I especially remember a Mexican American wedding party that I was invited to by a good friend, whose brother had just gotten married. Young and old danced together to lively guitar music. Plates, piled high with spicy tamales and enchiladas, filled the tables. The sounds of Spanish, spoken fast and mixed with laughter, filled the air. To me, the wedding guests seemed to revel in their togetherness.

Your interpretation is important. State what you think and then support it by explaining why you see it the way you do. Interpreting doesn't have to be "to" someone else. You can also ask the questions to yourself. In either case, it's a way of helping you understand your own opinions, thoughts, and feelings about what you read.

039 SYNTHESIZING

Synthesizing is the process of pulling pieces of information and ideas together. This is particularly important in your schoolwork.

When you pull together ideas from different sources, you create something new as you mix in your own ideas and experiences.

Example:

You read, think, and discuss:

You are interested in marriage, as a topic. You read about the research of Avshalom Caspi, a psychologist at the University of Wisconsin. You also read about the research of John Gottman, a psychologist at the University of Washington. You have your own observations to draw from; plus, you talk to your classmates.

Given what you know, you pull together something like this:

According to Avshalom Caspi, the secret to happiness in marriage is to marry someone like yourself. John Gottman, also a psychologist, believes it is the ability to handle differences, not similarity, that keeps spouses together. To me, these claims are compatible. To handle their differences, a couple has to create a shared style of communication. This means they are "alike" in at least one important aspect of their marriage. I once knew a couple who… .

Your teachers will expect you to do a lot of reading and pull it all together in your own unique way.

CREDITS

Photography

All photographs by Jonathan Stark with the exception of

p. 2 bottom	Dennis MacDonald/PhotoEdit
p. 7	AP/Wide World Photos
p. 34	Gabe Palmer/The Stock Market
p. 44 top	UNDERWOOD PHOTO ARCHIVES, SF
p. 44 bottom	Archive Photos/Potter Collection
p. 47	Cameramann/THE IMAGE WORKS
p. 58–62	Janet Lee Mills
p. 90 top	Alexandra Avakian/Woodfin Camp & Assoc.
p. 90 bottom	William Campbell/Time Magazine
p. 95	AP/Wide World Photos;
p. 96	Margaret Bourke-White/ Life Magazine
p. 103	The Bettmann Archive;
p. 104 left	UPI/Bettmann
p. 104 right	Paul Schutzer/Life Magazine
p. 106	The Granger Collection
p. 107	Gwendolyn Cates/SYGMA
p. 117–118	Barbara Y. E. Pyle
p. 130–131	Charlotte Thege/LINEAR
p. 145 top	Lionel J-M Delevigne/Stock, Boston
p. 145 bottom	David Bartruff/Stock, Boston
p. 150	Sammy Still/Cherokee Nation photographer
p. 171	JB Pictures
p. 181	Reuters/Bettmann

Illustration

Normand Cousineau: p. 199
Anne O'Brien: pp. 23, 48
Stephanie Peterson: unit, chapter, and strategy box decorations; pp. 75, 167, 207, 209, 225

Text